STAR WARS®
PANEL TO PANEL

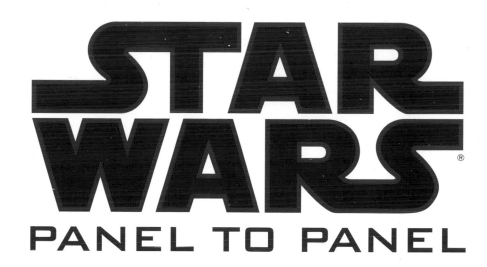

Art by Tsuneo Sanda.
Originally published as the wraparound cover of Star Wars 2002 Backlist Catalog.

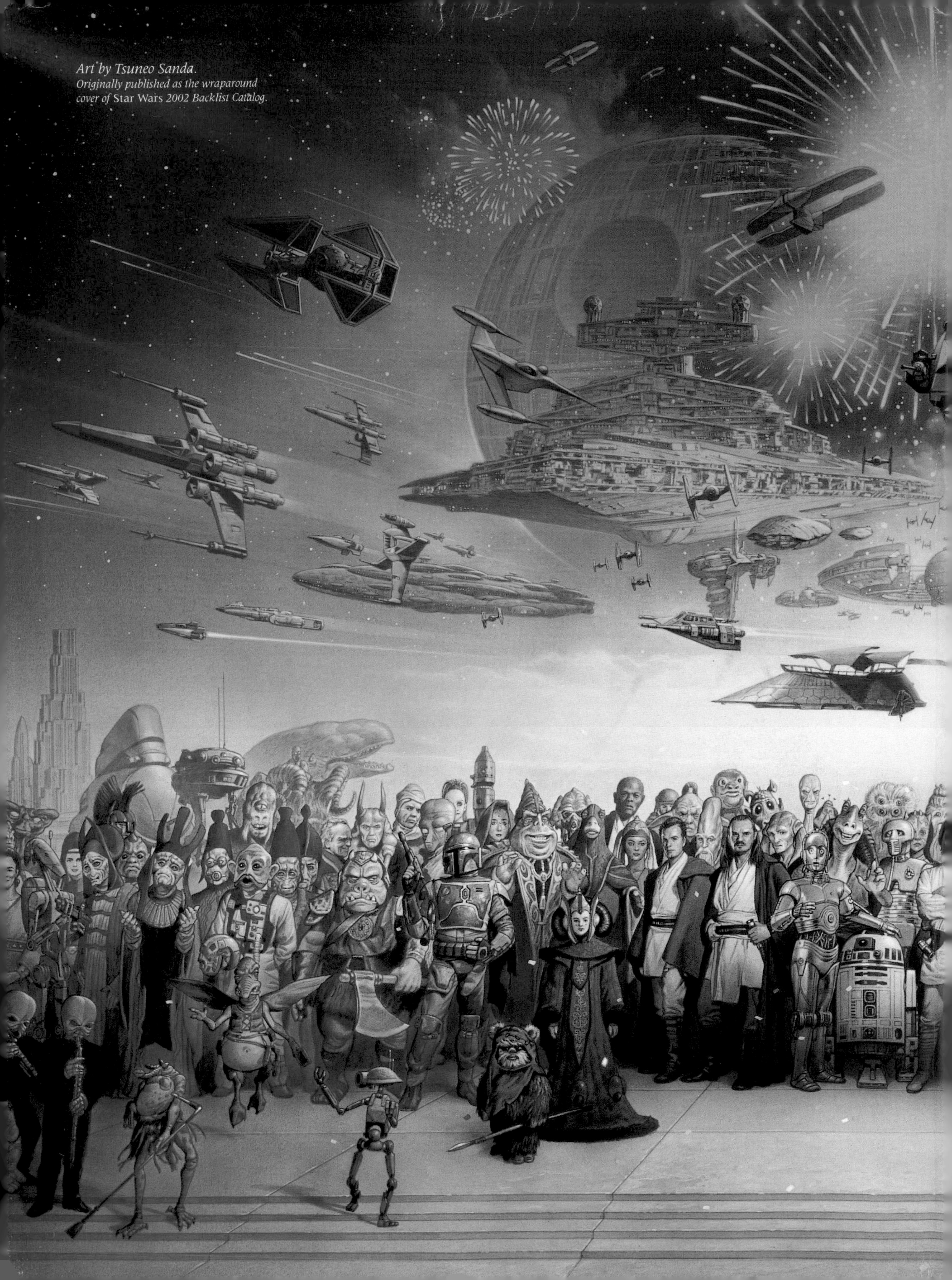

STAR WARS

PANEL TO PANEL

FROM THE PAGES OF DARK HORSE COMICS
TO A GALAXY FAR, FAR AWAY

TEXT BY
RANDY STRADLEY

DARK HORSE BOOKS™

TSUNEO SANDA

publisher
MIKE RICHARDSON

designer
LANI SCHREIBSTEIN

art director
LIA RIBACCHI

assisting editors
JEREMY BARLOW
MIKE CARRIGLITTO
DAVE MARSHALL

editor
RANDY STRADLEY

The editor gratefully acknowledges the assistance of Amy Gary, Sue Rostoni, Iain Morris,
Troy Alders, Leland Chee at Lucas Licensing, Dan Jackson at Dark Horse Comics,
and Lucy Autrey Wilson at JAK Productions.

Star Wars®: Panel to Panel

Published by Dark Horse Books, a division of Dark Horse Comics, Inc.

www.darkhorse.com
www.starwars.com

To find a comics shop in your area, call the Comic Shop Locator Service
toll-free at 1-888-266-4226

First edition: September 2004

ISBN 1-59307-261-9

3 5 7 9 10 8 6 4 2

Printed in China

TABLE OF CONTENTS

A WORD ABOUT THE CONTENTS

In December of 1991, Dark Horse Comics published *Star Wars: Dark Empire* #1—the first in what has become a long line of *Star Wars* comics and graphic novels. In the years since, comics writers and artists from all over the world have contributed to the *Star Wars* canon, telling and illustrating stories encompassing every era of the timeline, from adventures set thousands of years before the Prequel Trilogy, to tales extending well beyond the events in the Original Trilogy. For many of these time periods (and the worlds, species, and characters featured therein), the comics have been the only source for visual representations—and many of these illustrations have been quite spectacular. Until now, some of these images have never been seen except as comic-book covers plastered with logos, blurbs, and bar codes.

What we have endeavored to do here is provide a sampling of the best of the cover illustrations and interior pages from more than a decade of comics. Deciding which images to include from Dark Horse's nearly six hundred *Star Wars* publications has been no easy task. For several months, fellow editor Jeremy Barlow and I fussed first over boxes of comics and graphic novel collections, then over a mountain of photocopies, finally narrowing the selections down to what we thought was a reasonable, manageable stack. As I began to arrange the contents of this book page by page, it became clear that our "manageable stack" contained far more material than for which I had space. I'm sure, many readers will have favorites that do not appear within. Given that there were so many beautiful and compelling images from which to choose (with more images arriving for our current line of comics almost every day!), and only so much space available, cuts had to be made. If this volume is deemed successful, perhaps some day there can be another. For those pieces that have been included, we have credited the artist(s), and indicated where and when the piece was originally published and, if applicable, in which graphic novel collection it can currently be seen. Where story pages have been presented, the writers have also been credited.

Involving nearly as much discussion as what would be included in this book was how the material would be presented. Should the images be arranged chronologically according to their place in the *Star Wars* timeline? Or, should they appear in the order in which they first saw print? Either of these methods had its own set of drawbacks. Placed along the timeline of a galaxy far, far away, those characters with whom readers would be most familiar would not appear until the latter part of the book. Arranged in publication sequence, characters and scenes from vastly different eras would appear side-by-side with no apparent rhyme or reason. Finally, we decided upon grouping images according to their subject matter: heroes, villains, alien worlds, and so on. This method still left us with a few interesting juxtapositions, but it succeeded in highlighting the ebb and flow of the recurring themes upon which the *Star Wars* saga is built.

For those readers curious to know exactly when certain stories take place, or for those interested in further exploring the rich galaxy of *Star Wars* comics and graphic novels, a *Star Wars* timeline is included at the end of this book.

Randy Stradley
April 2004

HEROES AND ALLIES

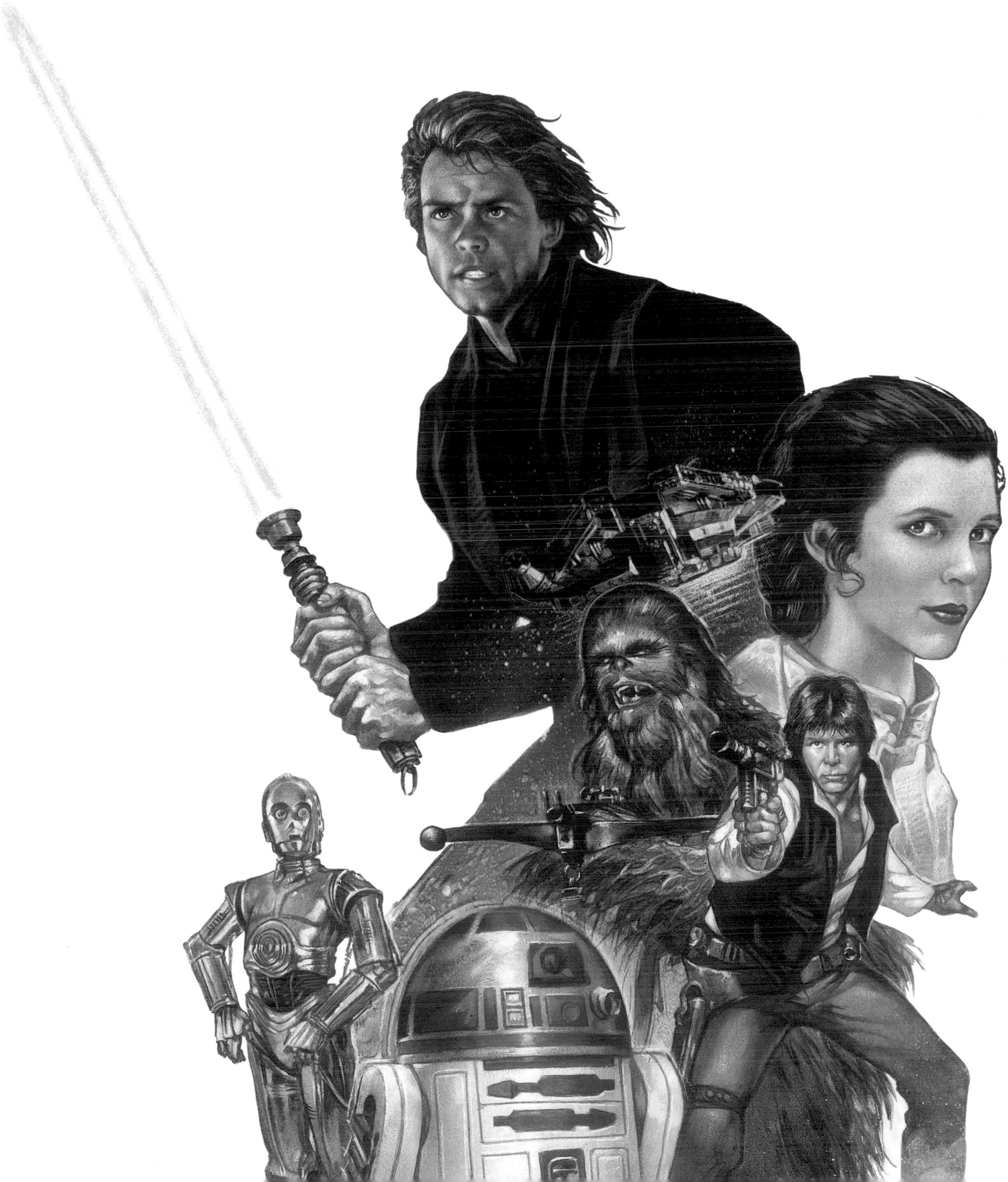

LUKE SKYWALKER

Farm boy … dreamer … pilot … Jedi.

Luke Skywalker is the quintessential hero; the Everyman driven by his own sense of justice, yet fated by his heritage to stand at the crux between the destruction of a galaxy–or its salvation. In his choices we see reflected our hopes, in his abilities our desires. So, he didn't get the girl in the films—it turned out she was his sister, anyway. But he did get the lightsaber, the coolest spaceship, and he got to blow up the Death Star!

Previous page: art by Dave Dorman, a reworking of his original cover for Dark Empire #1. Originally published as part of the cover of Wizard Ace Edition #13 (1997), a promotional comic book given away with issue #67 of Wizard magazine.

Nobody likes their heroes to be too sure of themselves—at least not at first. Growing up on Tatooine, Luke had plenty of opportunities to question himself, but he always did the right thing.

Script by Paul Chadwick, art by Doug Wheatley, colored by Chris Chuckry. Originally published in Empire #8 *(2003). Collected in* Empire Volume 2.

In 1994, when Dark Horse re-printed the movie adaptations originally published by Marvel Comics, new covers were commissioned—providing an opportunity for a new generation of comics artists to produce these interpretations of classic scenes.

Art by Arthur Adams, colored by Matthew Hollingsworth. Classic Star Wars: A New Hope #1 (1994).

Art by Adam Hughes, colored by Matthew Hollingsworth. Classic Star Wars: A New Hope #2 (1994).

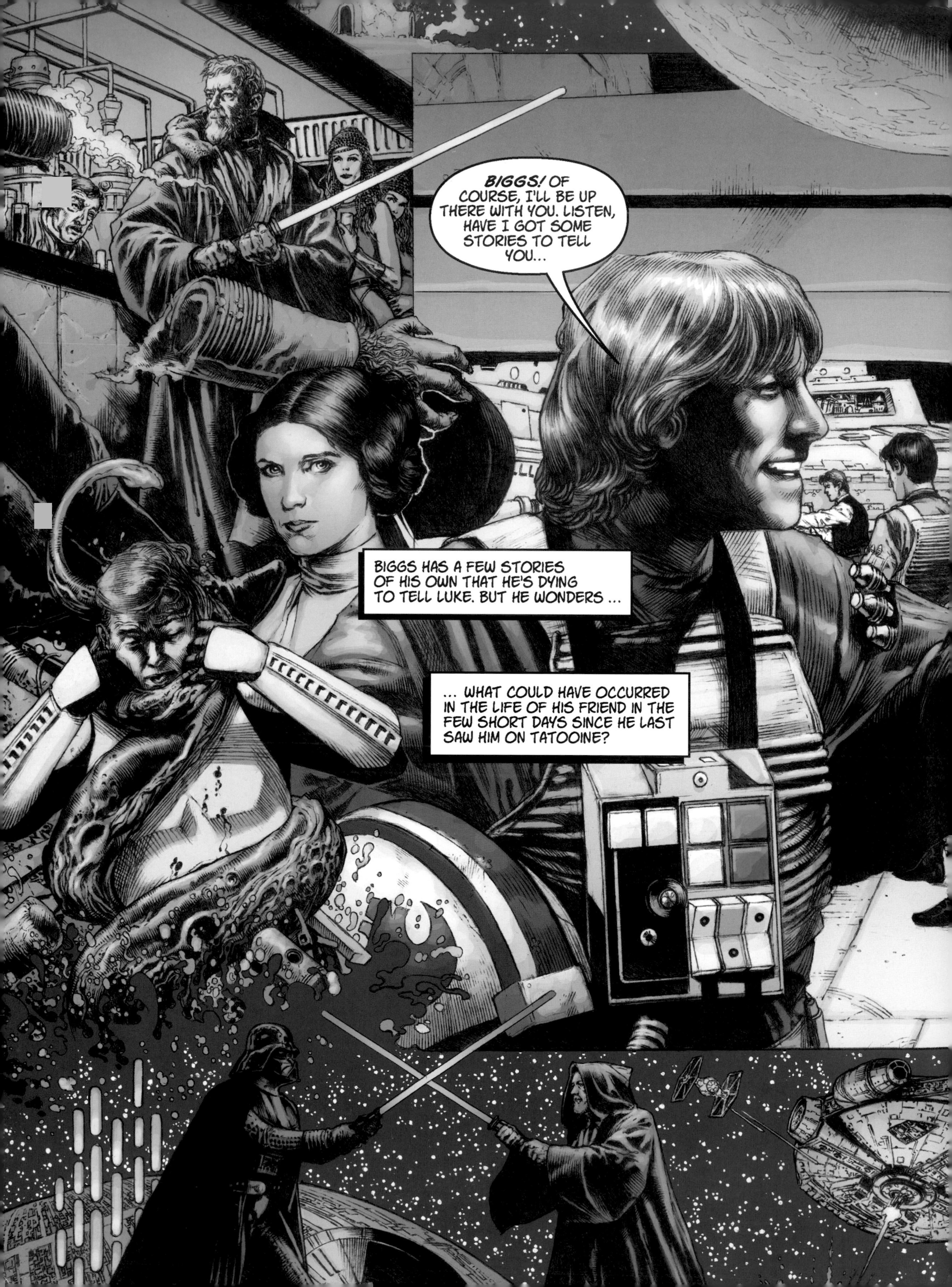
BIGGS! OF COURSE, I'LL BE UP THERE WITH YOU. LISTEN, HAVE I GOT SOME STORIES TO TELL YOU...
BIGGS HAS A FEW STORIES OF HIS OWN THAT HE'S DYING TO TELL LUKE. BUT HE WONDERS ...
... WHAT COULD HAVE OCCURRED IN THE LIFE OF HIS FRIEND IN THE FEW SHORT DAYS SINCE HE LAST SAW HIM ON TATOOINE?

WHAT BROUGHT LUKE HERE ... TO THE REBEL STRONGHOLD ON YAVIN 4?

BUT EVENTS PRESS ON THEM, AND SOON IT IS ESTABLISHED THEY'LL BE FLYING *TOGETHER*.

BIGGS IS *RED THREE* AND LUKE, *RED FIVE*.

Previous® page: Though most of the footage shot for *Star Wars: A New Hope* involving Luke's boyhood friend Biggs Darklighter ended up on the cutting room floor, those scenes were resurrected and expanded upon to reveal that Biggs' path to joining the Rebel Alliance was nearly as adventurous as Luke's. **This page:** in 1997, when the Special Editions of the original trilogy were released, Dark Horse commissioned all new art for a retelling of *A New Hope*.

Previous page: Script by Paul Chadwick, art by Doug Wheatley, colored by Chris Chuckry. Originally published in Empire #15 (2003). Collected in Empire *Volume 2.*
This page: Art by Dave Dorman. A New Hope—Special Edition, *issue #4.*

Luke and Leia crash landed on Circarpous V in one of the earliest *Star Wars* novels, *Splinter of the Mind's Eye* (1978), by Alan Dean Foster. The story was adapted to comics in 1995. This image appeared on the cover in issue #1 of the series.

Art by Duncan Fegredo for the collected Splinter of the Mind's Eye, *1996.*

Art by Duncan Fegredo. Shadows of the Empire—Evolution #3 *(1997).*

Shortly® before Dark Horse began publishing *Star Wars* comics, a new series of novels by Timothy Zahn hit the bookstores. Expanding on these immensely popular novels (*Heir to the Empire*, *Dark Force Rising*, and *The Last Command*), the comics series *Dark Empire* revealed the exploits of Luke, Leia, and the others in the years following *Return of the Jedi*. Eventually, Dark Horse published comics adaptations of the novels, as well.

Art by Mathieu Lauffray. Heir to the Empire *#1 (1995).*

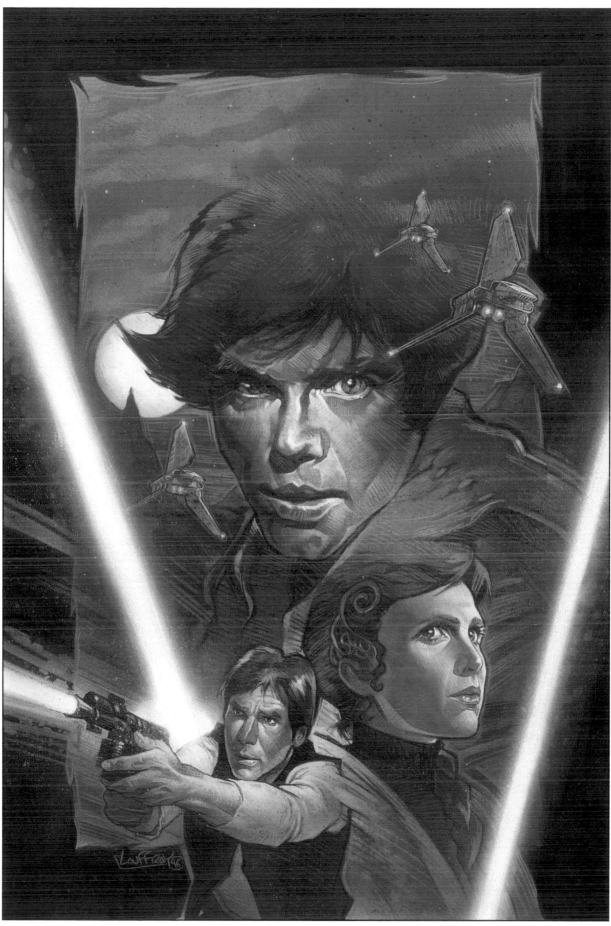

Next pages: For a time, resurrecting the Emperor and supplying the Empire with ever more powerful super weapons seemed to be requisite elements for new *Star Wars* stories. But it was Luke nearly succumbing to the dark side of the Force that held readers' attention in the *Dark Empire* trilogy. By this point in the storyline, Han and Leia were husband and wife, and expecting their third child.

This page: art by Mathieu Lauffray. Dark Force Rising *#2 (1997). Next pages: art by Dave Dorman. Wraparound cover for the collected* Dark Empire, *second edition (1995).*

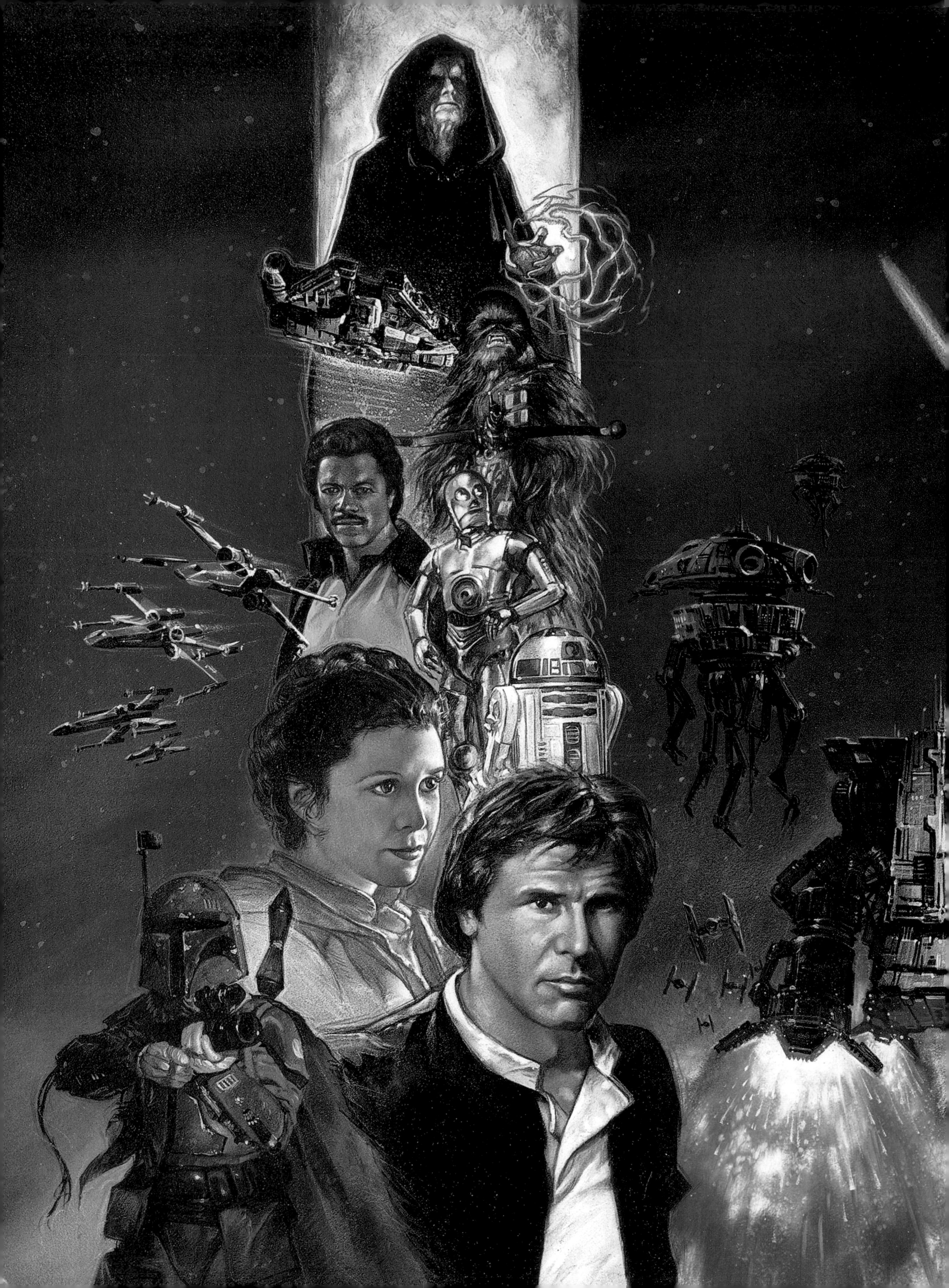

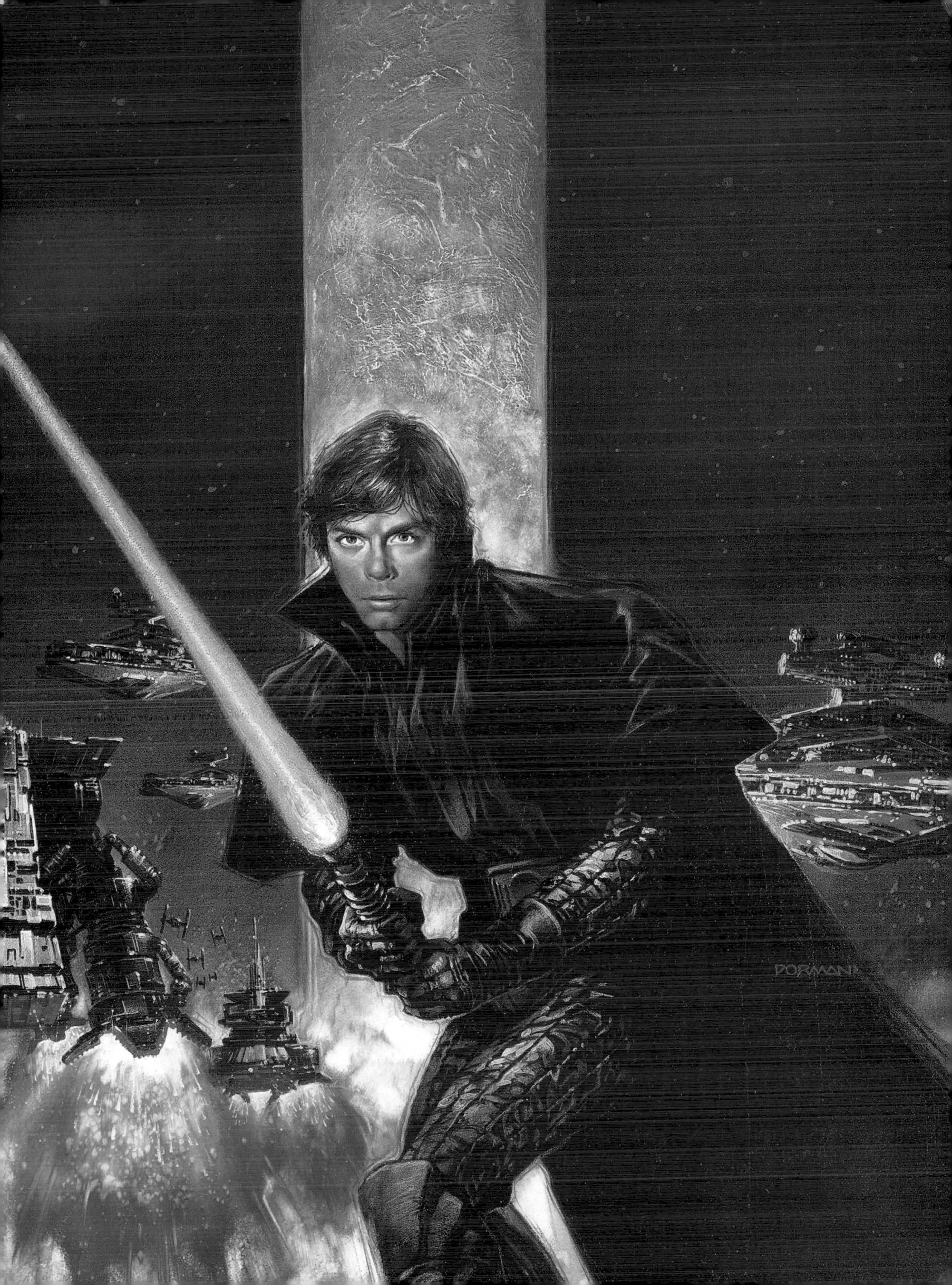
DORMAN

Did we mention that Luke nearly succumbed to the dark side?

Luke found true love—with the former Imperial assassin and one-time dark side adept Mara Jade.

Script by Mike Stackpole, art by Robert Teranishi, colored by Chris Chuckry. From Union *#3 (2000), collected in* Union *(2000).*

LEIA ORGANA

Without her raw courage, well-timed sarcasm, and strong leadership, the Rebel Alliance might never have won the all-important victory at Yavin. She rarely flew a spaceship, and she didn't own a lightsaber, but there's no doubt that Leia was the heart of the Rebellion. By the time the secret was revealed, it was easy to believe that Leia was Luke's twin. The Force was strong in her, but it manifested itself in her ability to lead and inspire rather than in martial prowess. Still, she was no slouch with a blaster—as she proved many times. And eventually she got to let her hair down…

Leia as she was when we were first introduced to her...

Art by Brian Stelfreeze. Star Wars #0: American Entertainment Exclusive *(1997), a promotional issue reprinting a story from* Pizzazz *magazine (1978).*

...and as the male fans will always remember her.

Art by Adam Hughes. Classic Star Wars: Return of the Jedi #1 (1994).

After the Battle of Yavin, Leia was in demand as a spokesperson for the Alliance, helping to recruit new systems to the Rebellion. While diplomacy was her strong suit, she was well versed in other methods of persuasion.

Stranded® in the icy wastelands of the planet Hoth, Leia and Han shared tender feelings for one another, as well as body heat.

Art by Paul Chadwick. Star Wars: A Valentine Story *(2003).*

In 1996, Dark Horse joined LucasArts, Ballantine Books, Hasbro Toys, and other *Star Wars* licensees in *Shadows of the Empire*, an organized exploration of the previously untold events that occurred between the end of *The Empire Strikes Back* and the beginning of *Return of the Jedi*. Here Leia and Chewbacca have disguised themselves as bounty hunters to infiltrate the criminal organization Black Sun. Note that Leia is wearing the "Boushh" disguise she uses to gain entry to Jabba's palace in *Return of the Jedi*.

Art by Hugh Fleming. Shadows of the Empire #4 (1996).

Even pregnancy couldn't keep Leia on the sidelines when duty called.

Art by Kilian Plunkett. Cover for the collected Star Wars: Dark Force Rising *(1998).*

Though Leia considered following in Luke's footsteps and becoming a Jedi, she realized the New Republic was better served by her political experience than her fencing skills.

HAN SOLO, CHEWBACCA, AND OTHER HEROES

Left to their own devices, they might never have become more than the rogues or buffoons they already were. But once they crossed paths with Luke and Leia, they were swept up in the spirit of freedom and became themselves shining lights of the Rebellion. In fact, it was their rough edges and sometimes reluctant —sometimes blundering—heroics that endeared them to us. Though we might wish for the stoicism of a Jedi, we know in our hearts that we might really be a Han, Lando, or Chewie—or even a Threepio.

Han Solo. His name suggests a loner, but Han rarely went anywhere without Chewbacca by his side. Theirs was a relationship that defied expectations, and it was obvious there was a brotherhood present that went far beyond the necessity to complete the next smuggler's run.

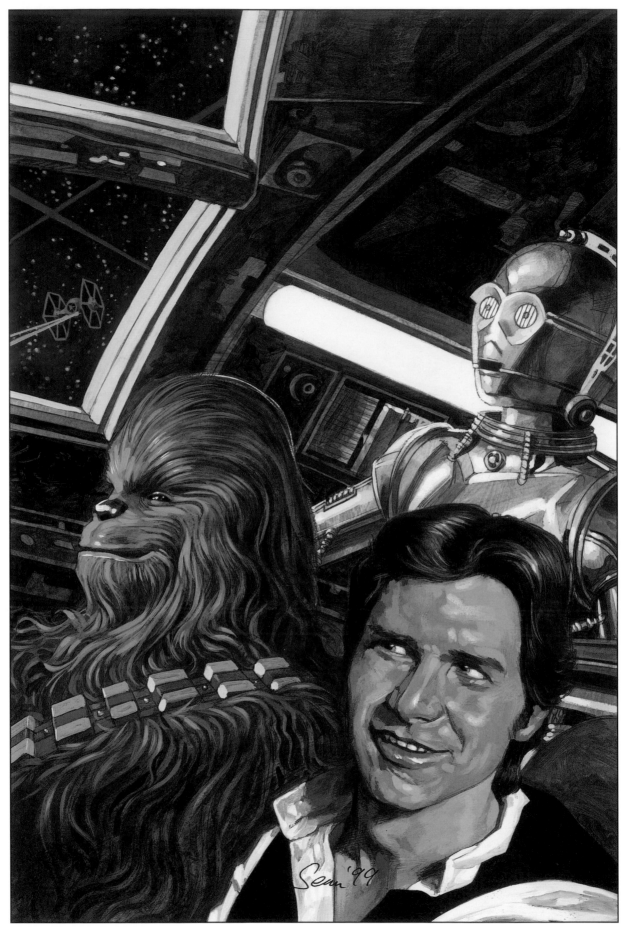

As much a part of the team as either Han or Chewie was the *Millennium Falcon*. The souped-up Corellian freighter was a smuggler's dream machine. She once belonged to Lando Calrissian, who lost her in a bet to Han.

The ship's bridge and hold became the setting for numerous pivotal scenes in the *Star Wars* mythos, and artists quickly realized that even a portion of her distinctive, sectioned front viewport was enough not only to establish the setting, but to evoke in the viewer the thrill of *Star Wars*-style space travel.

Art by Igor Kordey. The cover to issue #1 of the comics adaptation of Brian Daley's novel Han Solo at Stars' End *(1997).*

When audiences were first introduced to the galaxy's greatest smuggler, he had a price on his head. His "wanted" status brought Han to the attention of the galaxy's greatest bounty hunter, Boba Fett—resulting in an adversarial relationship that continued for years to come, as this cover from an issue of *Dark Empire II* attests. This despite the fact that, in happier times, Han, Lando, and Fett had occasion to work together (facing page).

Art by Dave Dorman. Dark Empire II #4 (1995).

Art by Andrew Robinson, colored by Dave Stewart. Underworld: The Yavin Vassilika #1 (2000).

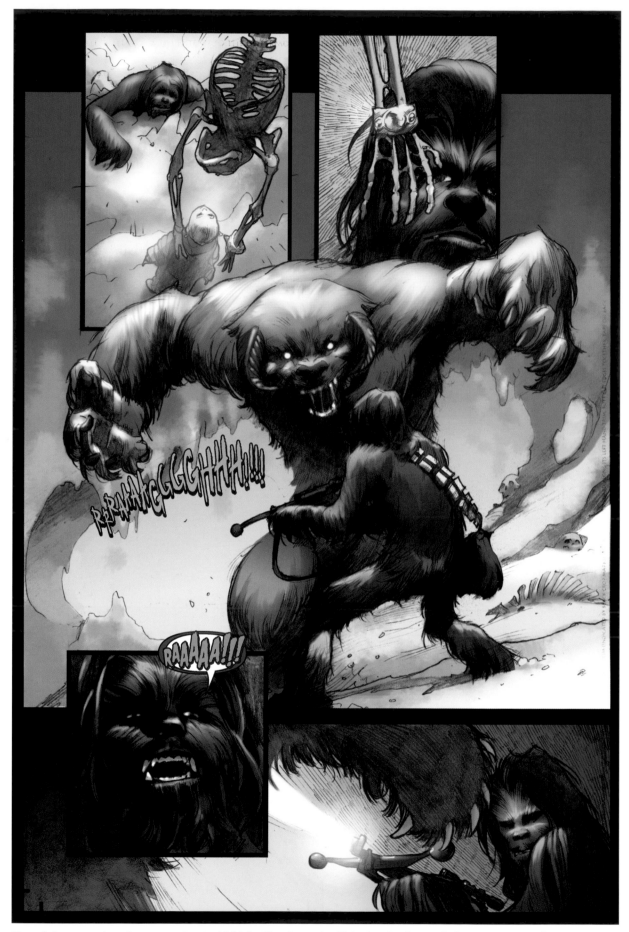

Though he was primarily seen as Han's sidekick, Chewbacca had his time in the spotlight, as in this confrontation with a wampa.

 Script by Rob Williams, art by Cary Nord, colored by Udon Entertainment. From "The Ghosts of Hoth," Star Wars Tales *#17 and collected in* Star Wars Tales *Volume 5 (2004).*

Chewbacca among his own kind.

Art by Mathieu Lauffray. Heir to the Empire #3 (1995).

A moment that rocked *Star Wars* fandom: Chewie dies. A scene that first occurred in R. A. Salvatore's New Jedi Order novel *Vector Prime*.

Script by Darko Macan, art by Rafael Kayanan, colored by Heroic Age. From Chewbacca *#4 (2000).*

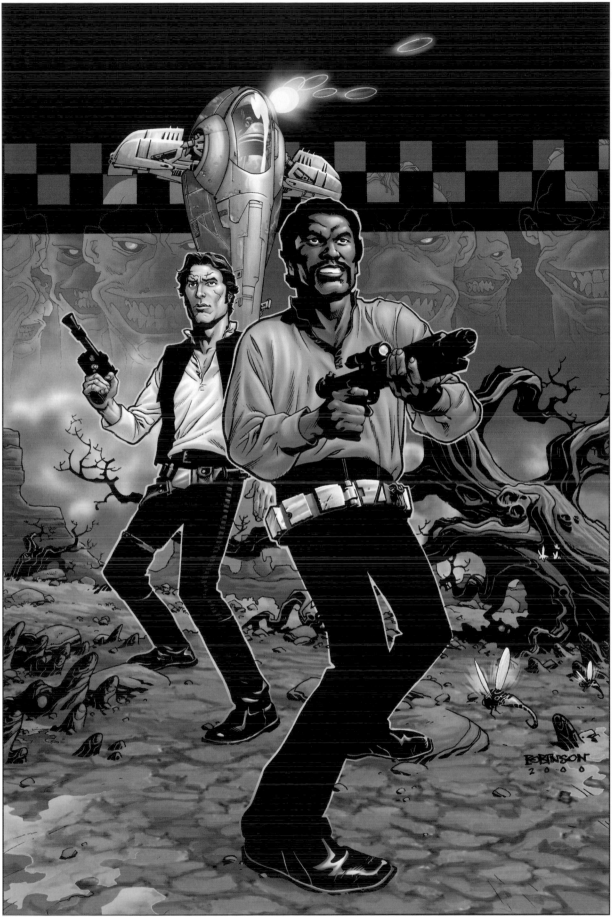

If anybody in the *Star Wars* galaxy could be called a jack of all trades, it was Lando Calrissian. He was, at one time or another, a gambler, the administrator of Cloud City, a general (and hero) in the Rebel Alliance, and a respected businessman—as much to his surprise and anyone else's.

Art by Andrew Robinson, colored by Dave Stewart. Underworld: the Yavin Vassilika #4 *(2001).*

Lando maintained his cool (well, almost) even when confronted by a rancor. R2-D2 remained the pluckiest droid in the galaxy. Unfortunately, even the *concept* of cool escaped C-3P0...

Innocents adrift or unwitting heroes?

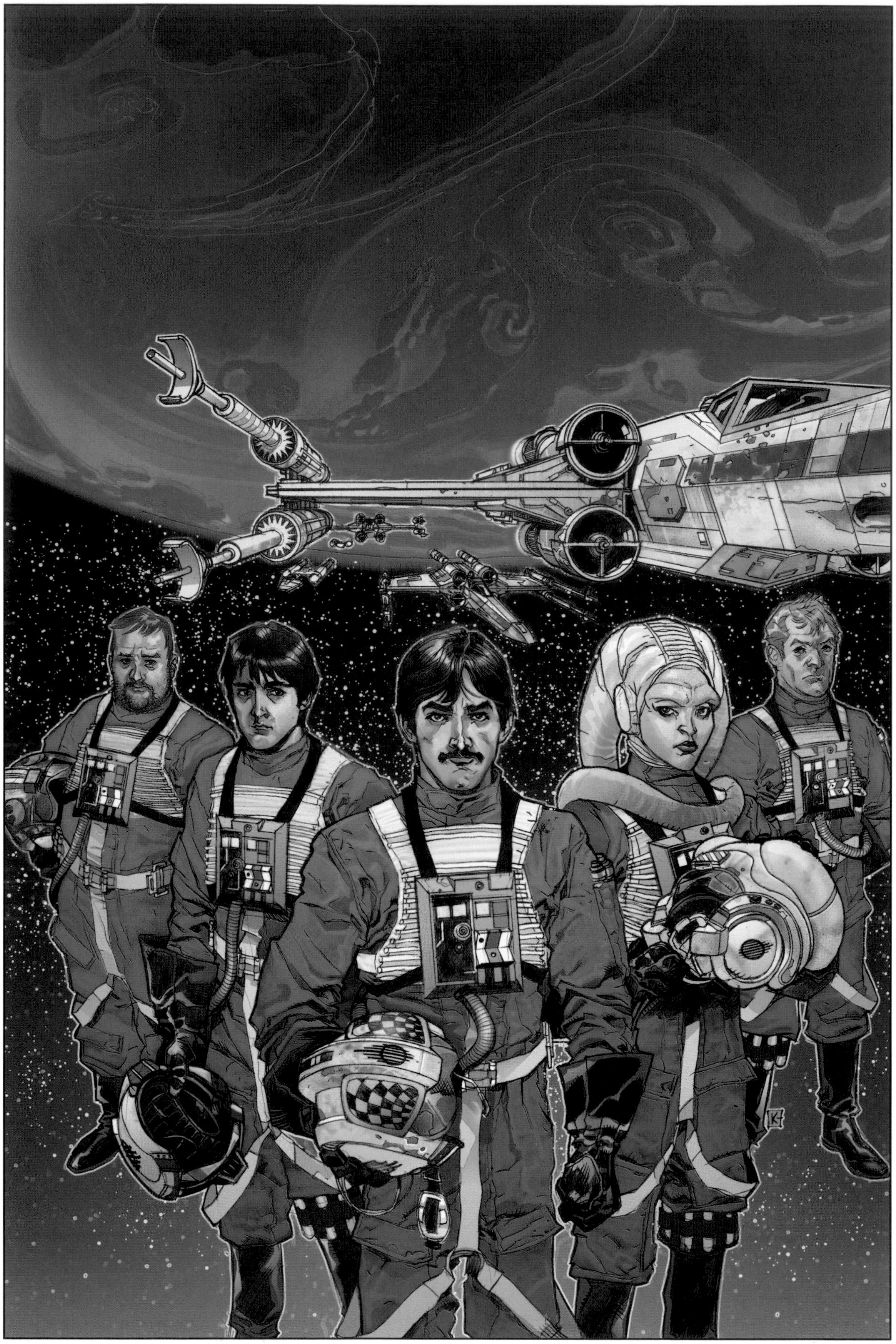

From left to right: Jek Porkins, Wedge Antilles, Biggs Darklighter, Cesi "Doc" Eirriss, and Garven Dreis—the members of Red Squadron ready for a mission that preceded the Battle of Yavin.

 Art by Kilian Plunkett. Empire *#12 (2003)—and the collection* Empire *Volume 2 (2004).*

Designated Red Two during the Battle of Yavin, Wedge Antilles went on to become one of the Rebellion's greatest pilots, and eventually a general for the New Republic. He is particularly famous for his role as commander of Rogue Squadron, the pilots who were often given the Alliance's most dangerous assignments.

Art by Dave Dorman. X-Wing: Rogue Squadron #1 (1995).

The future Mrs. Skywalker. Mara Jade, once known as "The Emperor's Hand," was Palpatine's foremost assassin. His death sent her on a hunt for Luke, unaware that she would eventually fall in love with the new leader of the Jedi.

Art by Mathieu Lauffray. Heir to the Empire #4 *(1996).*

Jar Jar Binks: blundering fool, inadvertent hero, and eventually a pawn of the Sith (Jar Jar was the one who proposed to the Senate that Palpatine be granted special, near-dictatorial powers at the onset of the Clone Wars).

OBI-WAN KENOBI AND ANAKIN SKYWALKER

They were the yin to each other's yang. Fans watched Obi-Wan grow from a Padawan learner to the consummate Jedi Master, and Anakin go from a slave boy to a powerful Jedi to, well, more on that later. But while they were together as Master and Padawan and as brothers in arms, they struck a balance that made them an unbeatable team. Obi-Wan listened to the voice of reason, Anakin heeded the call to action. From the planet-metropolis of Coruscant to the arena on Geonosis and back again, their exploits brought them to the attention of those in power … both good and evil.

After suffering a defeat by Obi-Wan early in the Clone Wars, dark Jedi Asajj Ventress became obsessed with destroying Kenobi—just as he became obsessed with bringing her to justice. In Ventress, Obi-Wan's fears that he was failing Anakin were made flesh.

Obi-Wan Kenobi fought many famous adversaries during his lifetime, including *three* Sith Lords: Darth Maul, Count Dooku, and Darth Vader. Here, and on the pages following, he fights his most notable non-Jedi opponent, the bounty hunter Jango Fett.

This page: art by Tsuneo Sanda. Following pages: script by Henry Gilroy, pencils by Jan Duursema, inks by Ray Kryssing, colored by Dave McCaig. Episode II: Attack of the Clones *(2002).*

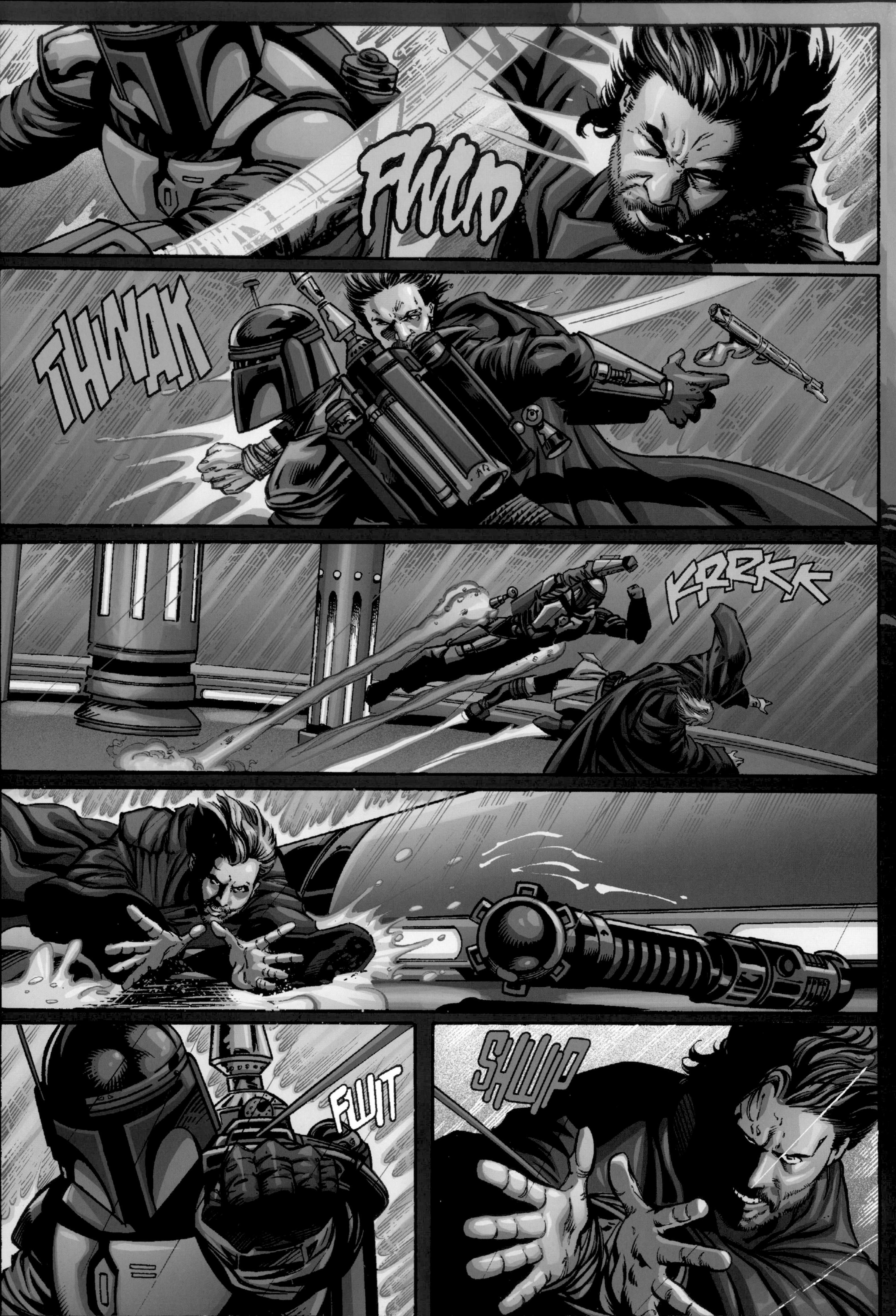
FWUD
THWAK
KRRKK
FWIT
SHWIP

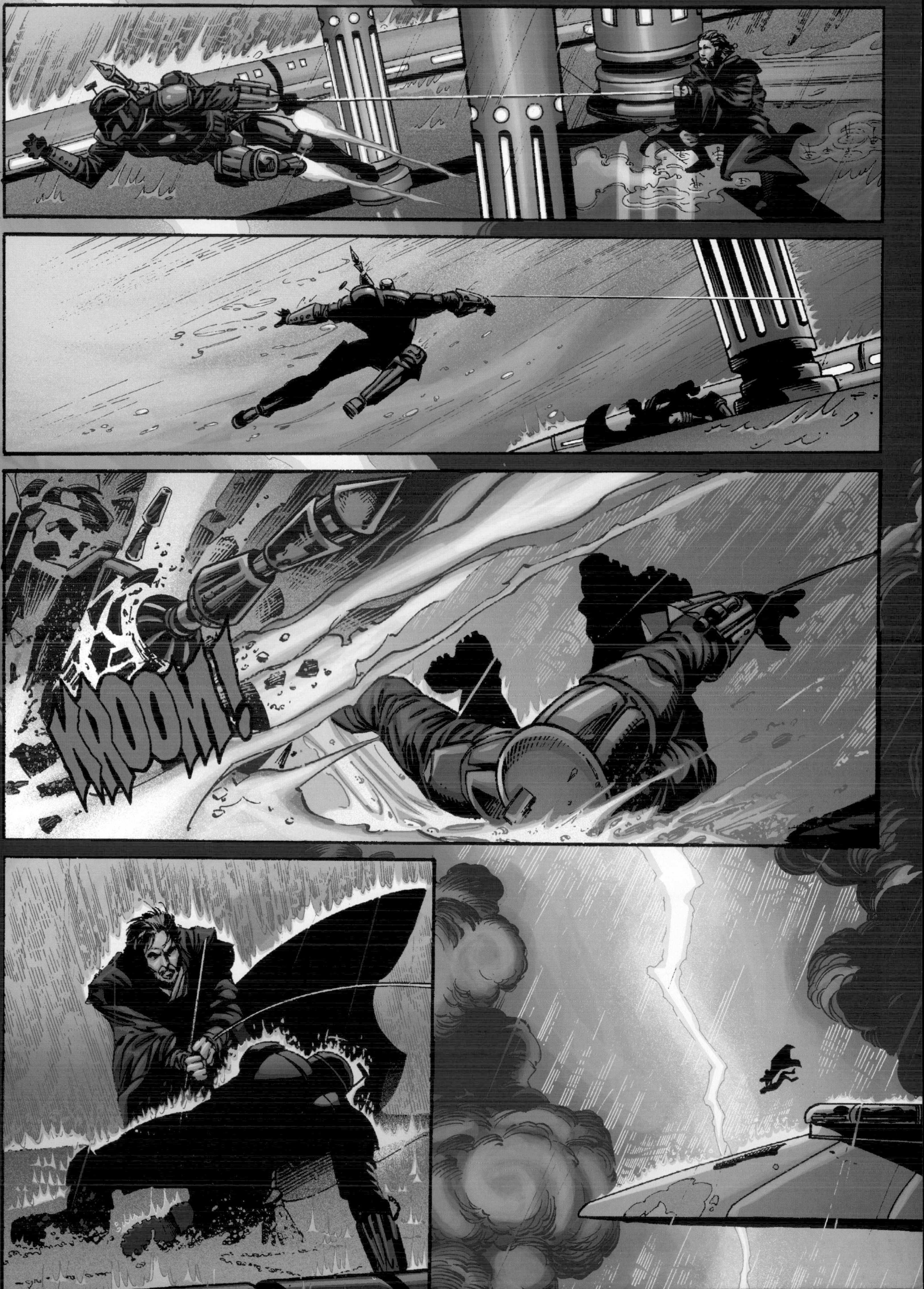
KROOM!

General Kenobi. After battling Jango Fett, Obi-Wan's next assignment had him leading an army of Jango's clones against the Separatists in the Clone Wars.

Twenty-some years later, Obi-Wan would find himself allied with new associates against an old enemy—and an old friend.

This page: Art by Mathieu Lauffray. The Last Command #1 (1997). *Next page: Art by Ravenwood. From the graphic novel* Episode I: The Phantom Menace *(1999).*

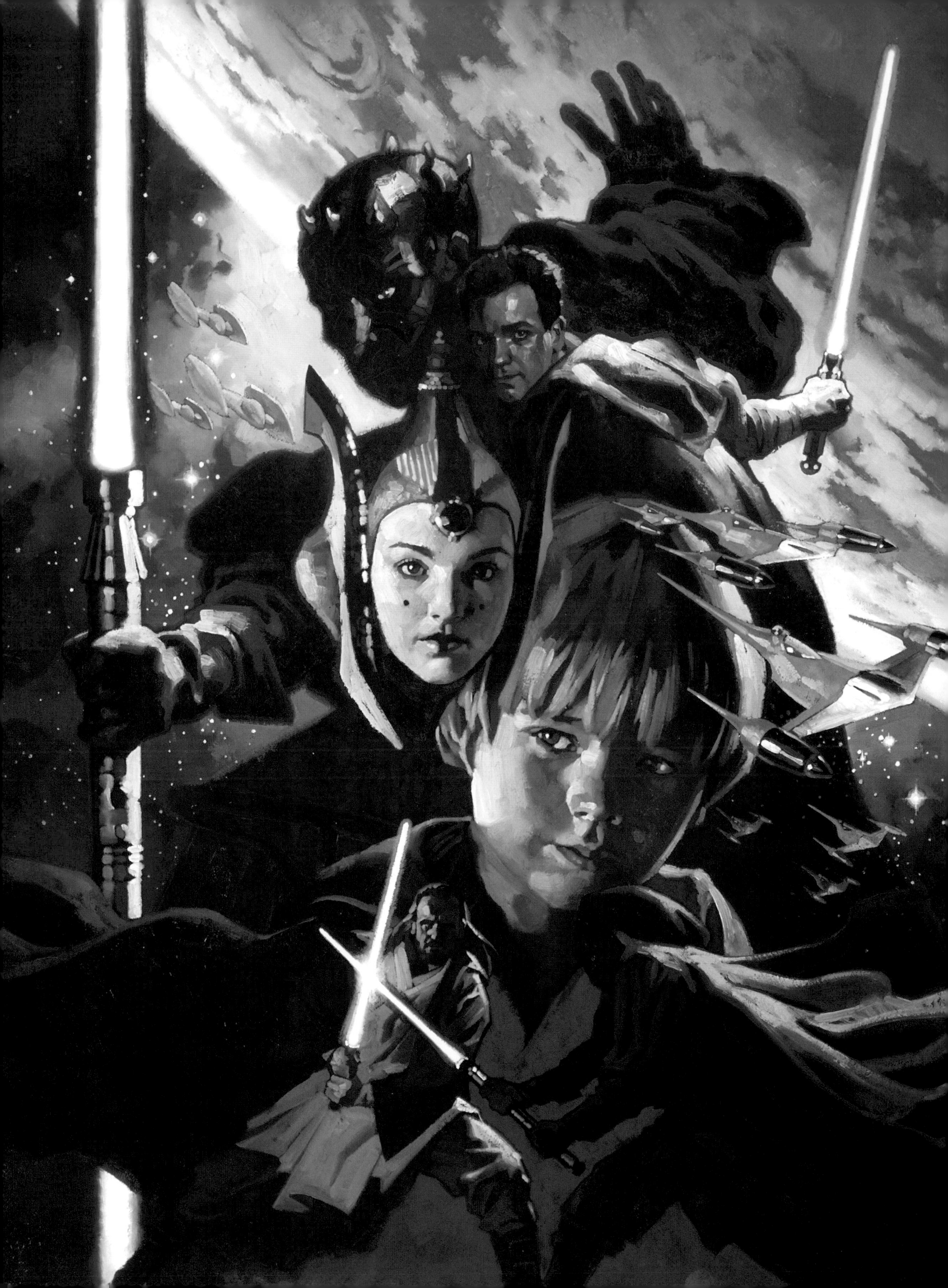

"Fear leads to anger... anger leads to hate... hate leads to suffering."

Top: script by Tim Truman, art by Robert Teranishi, colors by Chris Chuckry. Originally published in Episode I: Anakin Skywalker *(1999), collected in* Episode I Adventures *(2000). Bottom: script by John Ostrander, pencils by Jan Duursema, inks by Dan Parsons, colored by Brad Anderson. Originally published in* Republic #59 *(2003), collected in* Clone Wars Volume 3 *(2004).*

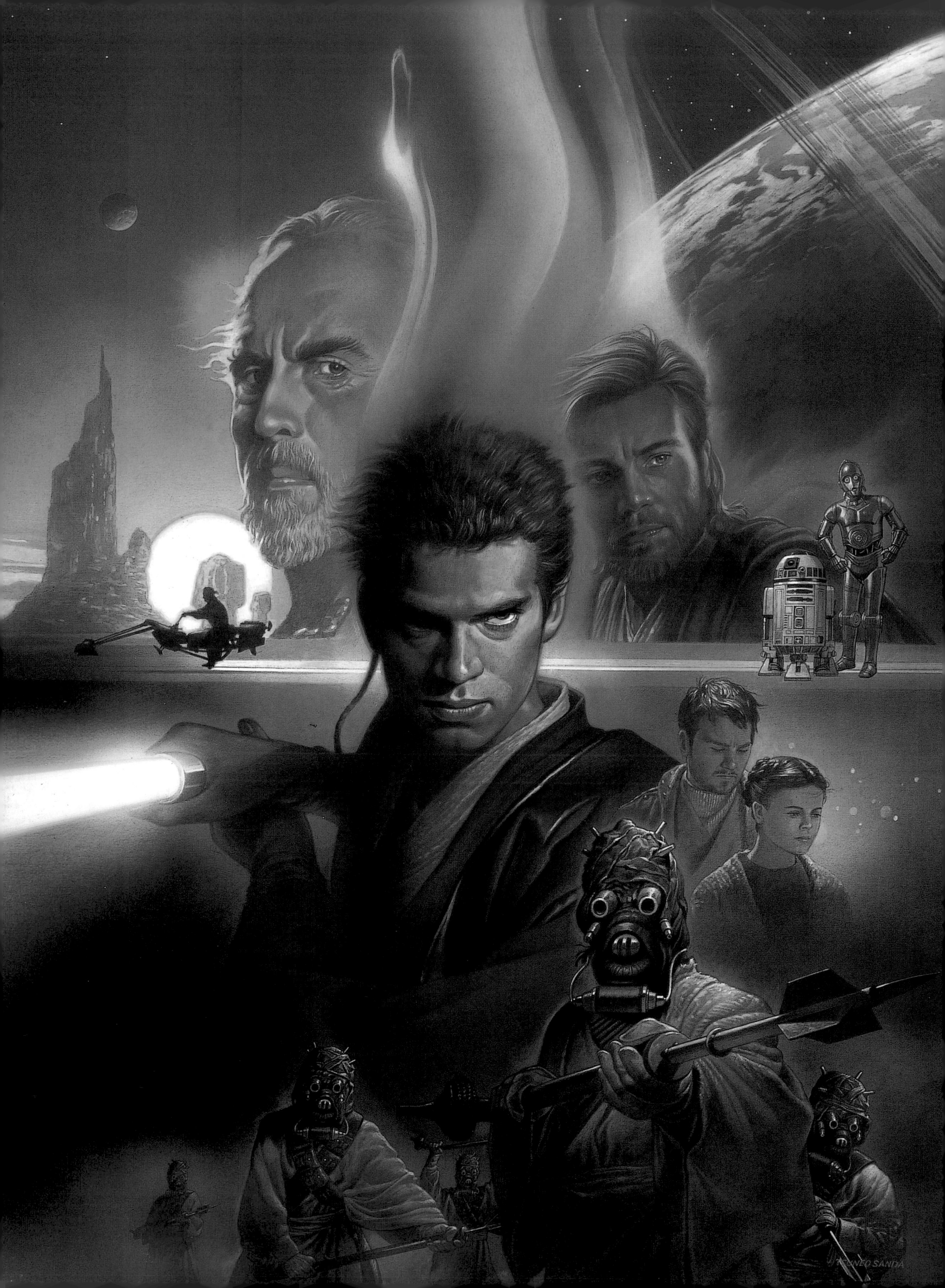
SANDA

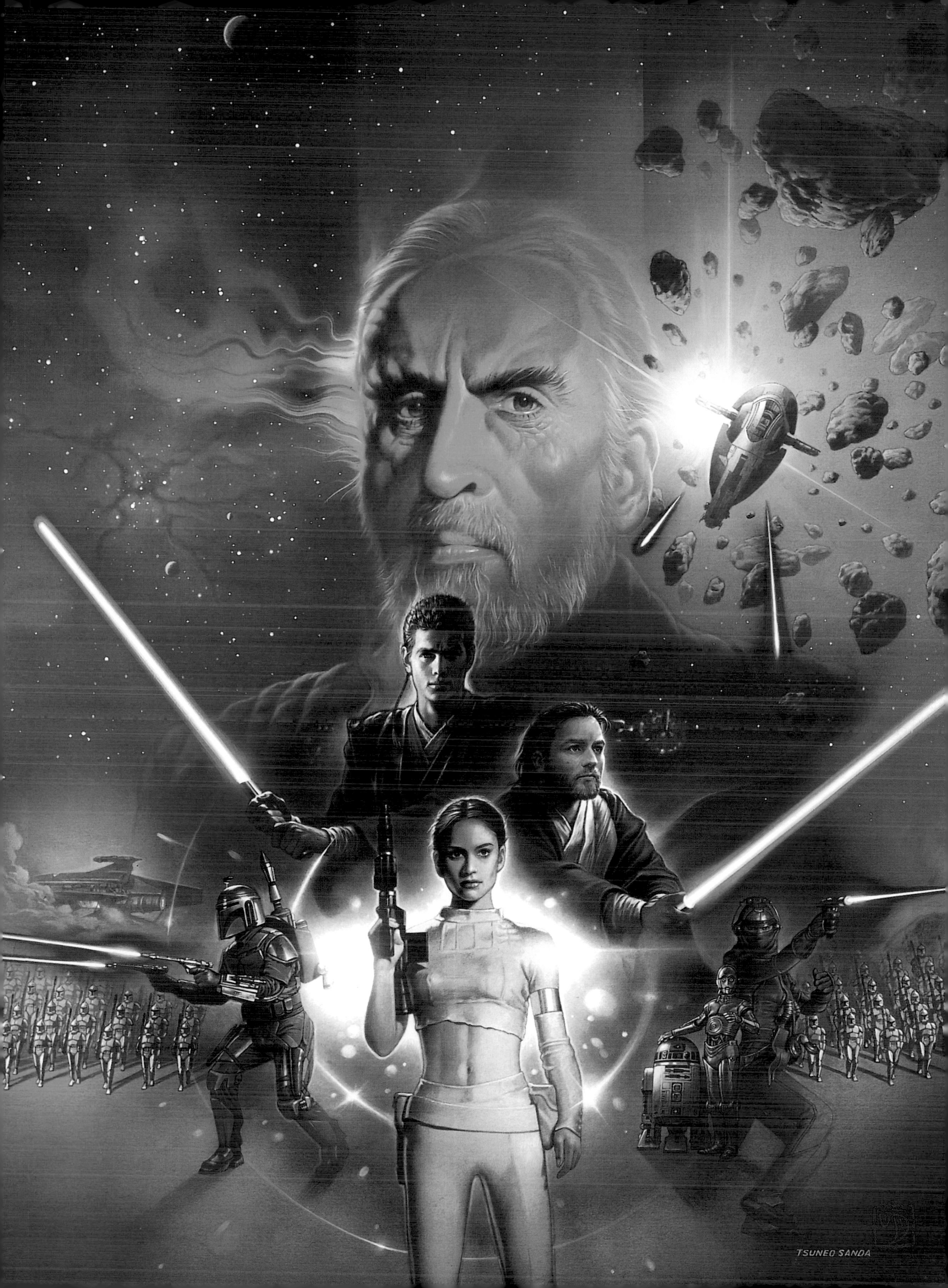
TSUNEO SANDA

Finding love, forbidden though it might be, seemed to soften Anakin…

Previous pages: art by Tsuneo Sanda. Episode II: Attack of the Clones, issues #3 and #4 (2002). Script by Henry Gilroy, pencils by Jan Duursema and Ray Kryssing, colored by Dave McCaig. Episode II: Attack of the Clones (2002).

…but the secret of it strained his friendship with Obi-Wan.

Pencils by Jan Duursema, inks by Ray Kryssing, colored by Brad Anderson. Originally published in Republic *#50 (2003), collected in* Clone Wars *Volume 1 (2003).*

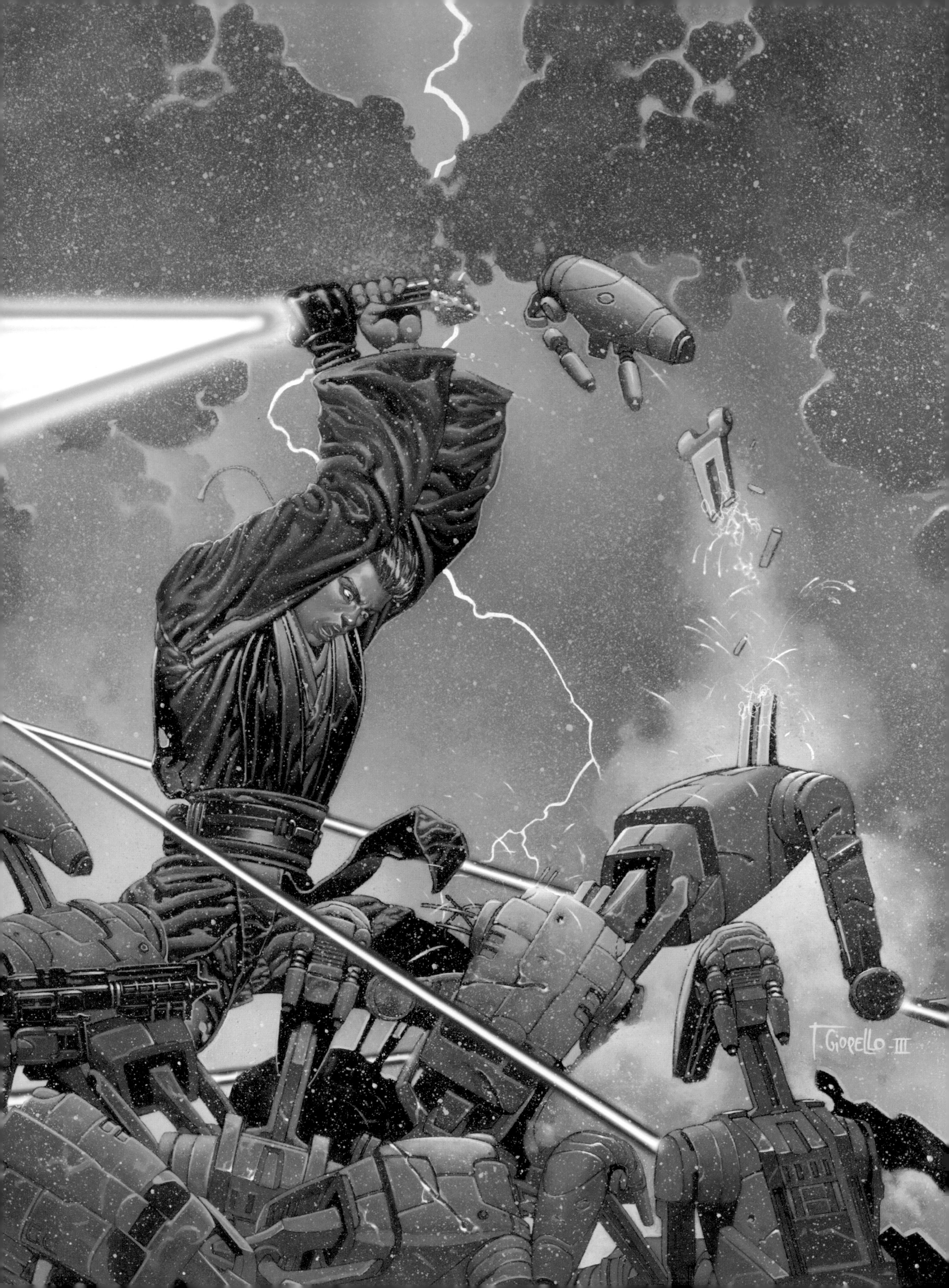
T. Giorello-III

Whether in victory, or in retreat, the Clone Wars took a heavy toll on the Jedi—physically and spiritually. None seemed so affected as Anakin.

Previous page: art by Tomás Giorello. Republic #56 (2003). This page: art by Jan Duursema, colored by Brad Anderson. Republic #58 (2003).

Before the fall.

Art by Brian Ching, colored by Brad Anderson. Republic #67 (2004).

VILLAINS AND ROGUES

DARTH VADER AND EMPEROR PALPATINE

One a boy of near-infinite potential—and boundless rage—steered and controlled from an early age by a master schemer and deceiver whose machinations destroyed a Republic that had stood for thousands of years. The other the deceiver himself, wily, deceptively meek, always pulling strings from behind the scenes, yet brooding and powerful in his own right. Bound to one another by their thirst for power, they ruled the galaxy—until the master tried to destroy the son the apprentice had just begun to know…

Previous page: art by Udon Entertainment. Star Wars Tales #17 (2003).

In a galaxy of iconic characters, there is one more instantly recognizable than any other; the icon's icon, if you will: Darth Vader. The story of *Star Wars* is Anakin/Vader's, after all, and every aspect of the character has become so closely associated with the mythos that Lucasfilm has used little more than Vader's labored, mechanical breathing in the soundtrack of the trailers for some of the films—that being enough to raise spontaneous applause from anticipatory audiences.

Art by Igor Kordey. Star Wars Tales #1 *(1999).*

That Anakin had built C-3PO from spare parts was not known when the original trilogy was first released. But the events in *The Phantom Menace* suggested new possibilities for a moment on Cloud City that was *not* revealed in *The Empire Strikes Back*.

Art by Kilian Plunkett, coloring by Jason Hvam. Star Wars Tales #6 (2000).

Script by Ryder Windham, art by Kilian Plunkett, coloring by Dave McCaig, lettering by Steve Dutro. From the story "Thank the Maker" in Tales #6, *later collected in* Star Wars Tales *Volume 2 (2002).*

69

Whether Vader is viewed in a moment of furious action…

Art by Brian Horton. Empire #3 (2002).

…or caught in a reflective pause…

Script by Ron Marz, art by Brian Ching, colored by Michael Atiyeh. Empire #19 (2004), collected in Empire Volume 3 *(2004).*

73

...there is never any question of his power. He *is* the Dark Lord.

Script by Ron Marz, art by Claudio Castellini, colored by Guy Major, lettering by Jason Hvam. From "Extinction" in Tales *#1 (1999), collected in* Star Wars Tales *Volume 1 (2002).*

Indeed, Vader's presence permeates the entire *Star Wars* saga.

Pencil art by Al Williamson, inks by Allen Nunis, colored by Gregory Wright. Classic Star Wars #3 (1992). *Next page: art by Doug Wheatley.* Empire #19 (2004).

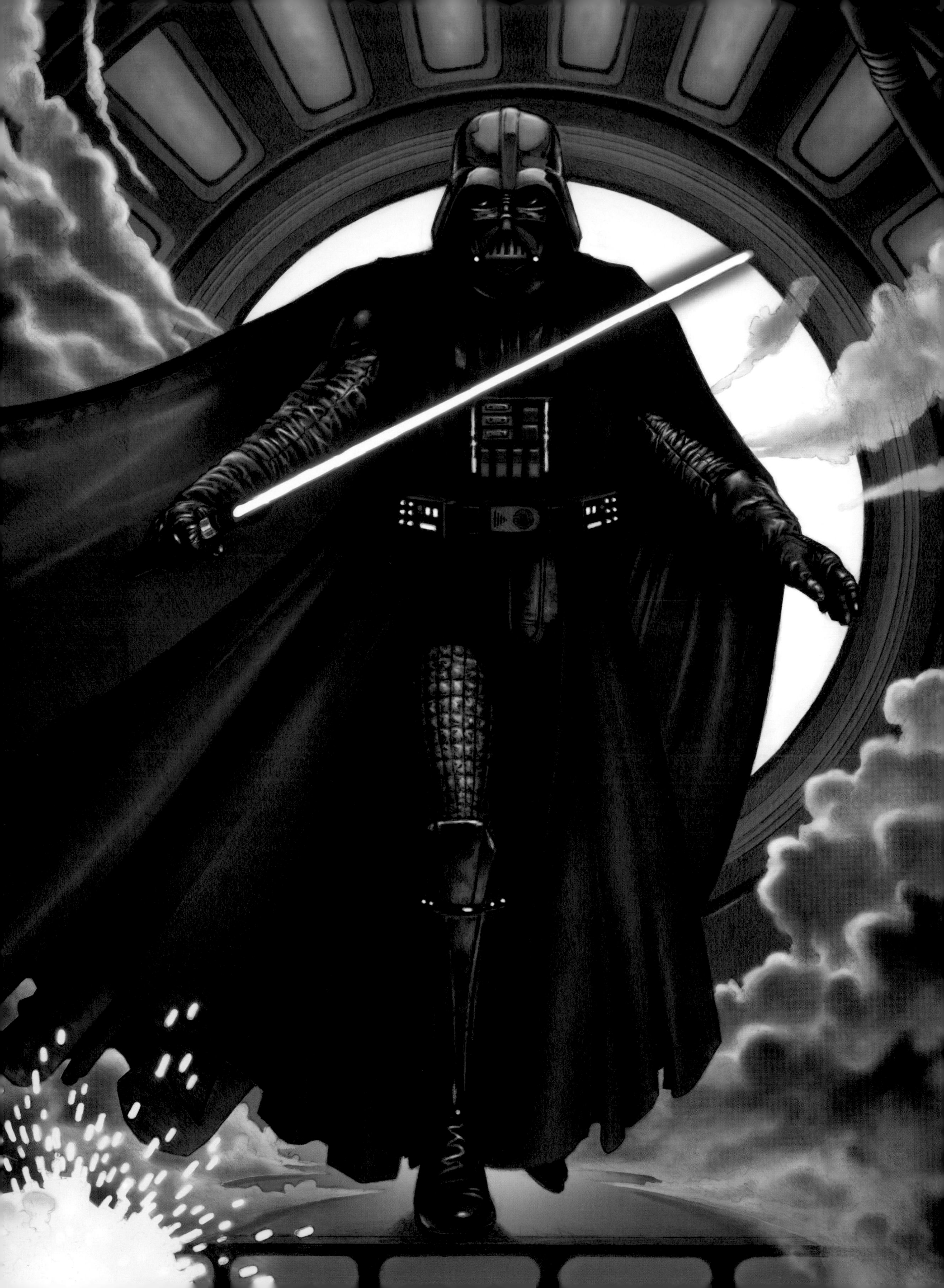

A face only a Sith could love. His visage ravaged by his tapping into the dark side of the Force, Palpatine's plan for galactic dominance was successful, but at a price.

Art by Dave Dorman. The background painting for the image that appears on page 7 of this book. Wizard Ace Edition #13 (1997), *a promotional comic book given away with issue #67 of* Wizard *magazine.*

From Senator to Emperor, Palpatine was always the master manipulator. From Jedi Masters to his own apprentices, no one was exempt from his "handling."

Top: script by John Ostrander, art by Brandon Badeaux, coloring by Brad Anderson, lettering by Michael David Thomas. From Republic *#64 (2004).* Bottom: *script by Scott Allie, pencils by Ryan Benjamin, inks by Curtis Arnold, coloring by Dave Stewart, lettering by Michelle Madsen. From* Empire *#1 (2002), collected in* Empire *Volume 1 (2003).*

And few understood power—or even the *trappings* of power—as well as Palpatine.

Script by Nathan Walker, art by Kilian Plunkett, colors by Dave Nestelle, lettering by Steve Dutro. From "First Impressions" in Star Wars Tales #15 (2003), *collected in* Star Wars Tales *Volume 4 (2004).*

Even after® his death in *Return of the Jedi*, Palpatine returned—as a cloned body inhabited by the Emperor's dark side spirit—to vex Luke, Leia, and the others. It wasn't until the events in *Empire's End* (set seven years after *Return of the Jedi*) that our heroes were finally rid of him.

Art by Dave Dorman. Empire's End #2 (1995).

SITH, GRAND MOFFS, AND OTHER MINIONS

On his path from politician to despot, Palpatine was surrounded by men, women, and aliens who turned his words into actions. Some embraced their master's goals of domination with greedy glee and became villains we could all love to hate. Others, possessing scant power or will of their own but existing in greater numbers, were ubiquitous symbols of the Empire—and cannon fodder in its war on freedom.

High on the list of popular villains is Darth Maul. Brooding and single-minded, quick to action and slow to speak, he was the embodiment of the Sith threat in *The Phantom Menace*. If writers and artists playing in George Lucas' sandbox, the Expanded Universe, have one universal regret, it is that Maul died too soon.

Art by Hugh Fleming. Episode I: The Phantom Menace #3 (1999).

In 2000, Dark Horse was fortunate enough to obtain the services of artist Drew Struzan—famous for producing the art for numerous film posters, including all of Lucasfilm's *Indiana Jones* series and several of the *Star Wars* films. His covers for the *Darth Maul* miniseries appear on the next four pages.

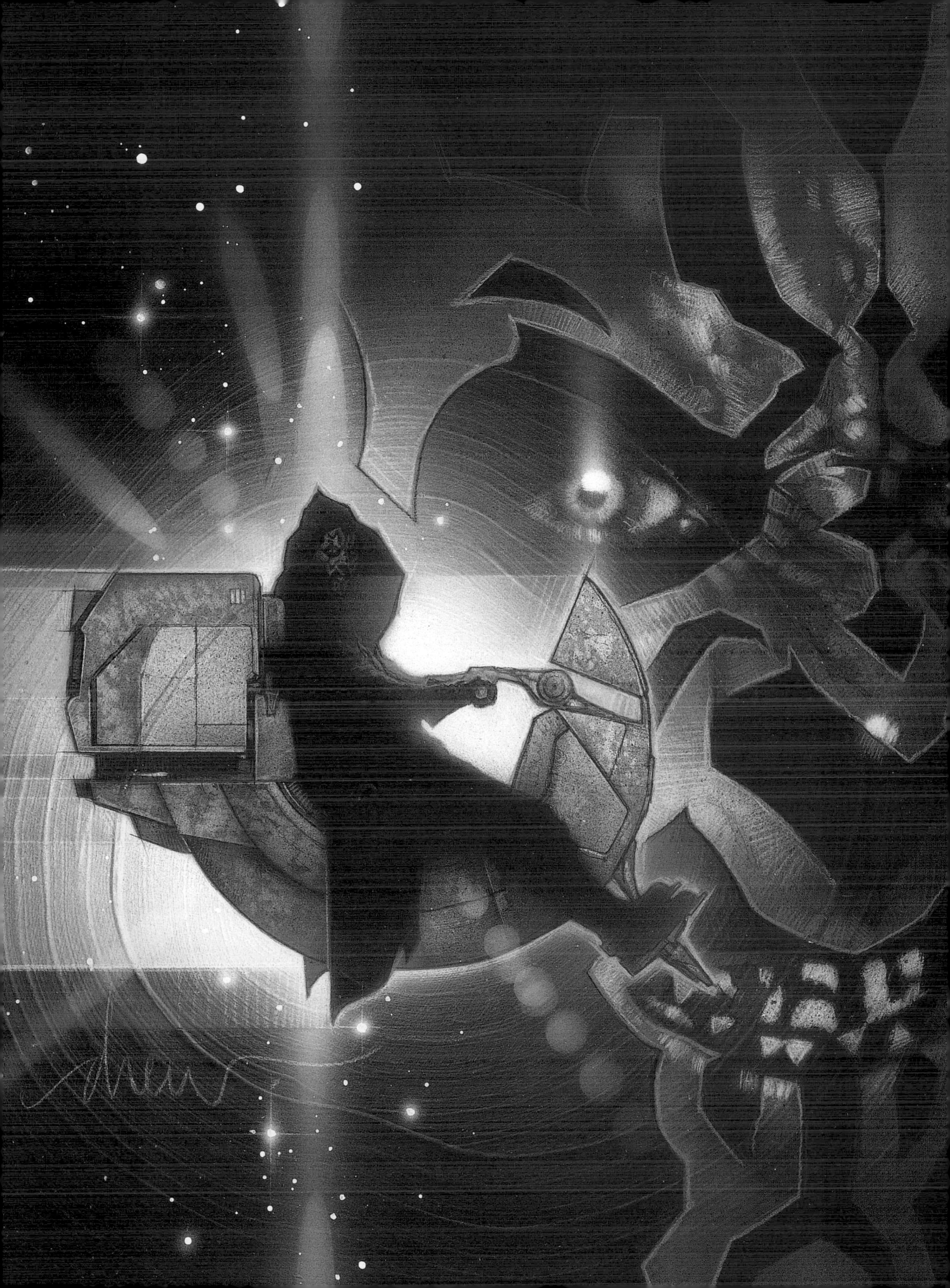

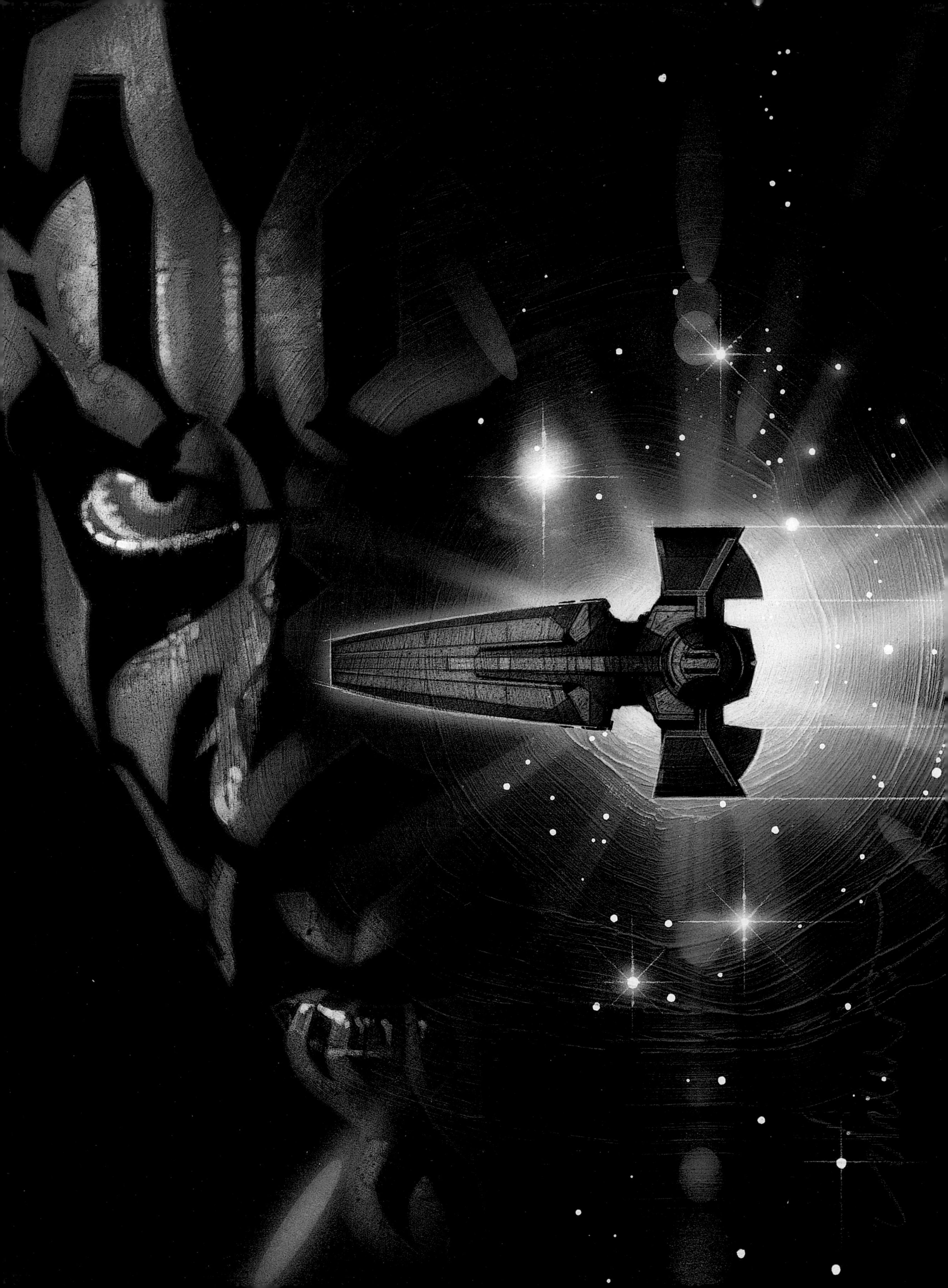

You didn't think Maul's tattoos stopped at his neck, did you?

This page® and facing: some of the action from the *Darth Maul* series. So hungry were comics readers and creators for more Maul that in 2001 Dark Horse produced an imaginary tale under Lucasfilm's *Infinities* label that twisted time and allowed Darth Maul and Darth Vader to fight one another for Sith supremacy. That story is collected in *Star Wars Tales* Volume 3.

Script Ron Marz, pencils Jan Duursema, inks Rick Magyar, colors Dave McCaig, lettering Steve Dutro. Collected in Darth Maul *(2003).*

Maybe if the Mon Calamarian says, "please"?

After Maul's demise in *The Phantom Menace*, Darth Sidious looked to the ranks of ex-Jedi for his next apprentice. More sophisticated, more calculating, and if anything deadlier than Maul, Count Dooku (a.k.a. Darth Tyranus) proved himself more than a match for the combined skills of Obi-Wan Kenobi and Anakin Skywalker in *Attack of the Clones*.

In *Attack of the Clones*, Dooku tried—unsuccessfully—to sway Obi-Wan to his dark path. In the stories told in the comics, Dooku had better luck with other Jedi, eventually surrounding himself with a cadre of dark Jedi who were anxious to do his evil bidding.

Some villains became heroes. Here we see the Empire's greatest pilot—Baron Fel—before his capture by, and defection to the Rebel Alliance. Fel epitomized the professional soldier, placing honor above duty. When the truth of the evil behind the Empire's rule became clear to him, he traded his TIE interceptor in for an X-wing and joined the Rebellion.

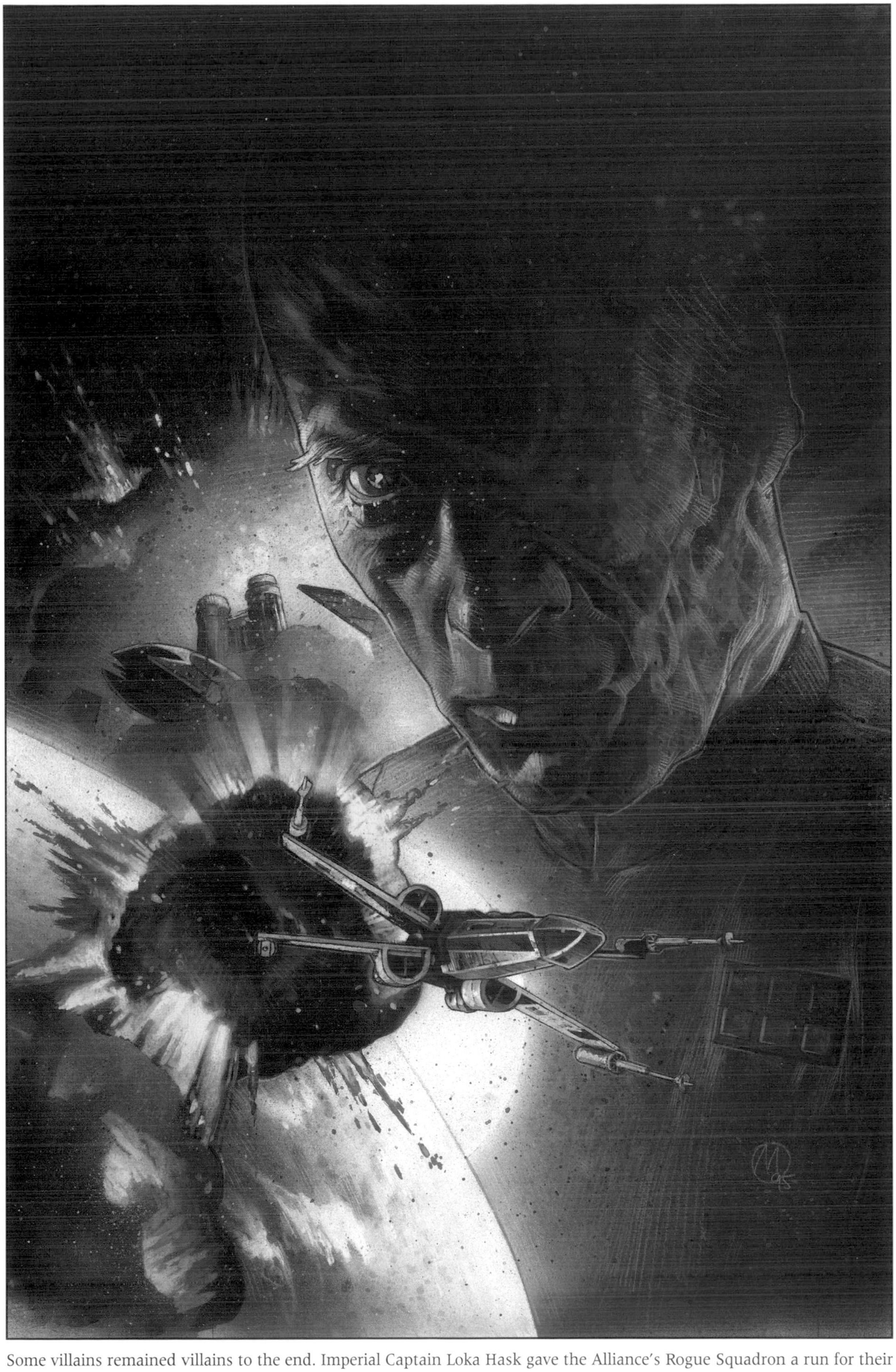

Some villains remained villains to the end. Imperial Captain Loka Hask gave the Alliance's Rogue Squadron a run for their money in their bid for a Mrlssti cloaking device.

As commanding as Dark Lords, Grand Moffs, and Imperial officers might be, the real day-to-day muscle of the Empire was its stormtroopers. Heavily armed, identical, and intimidating behind their helmet visors, they were everywhere the Empire needed them to be—usually *en masse*.

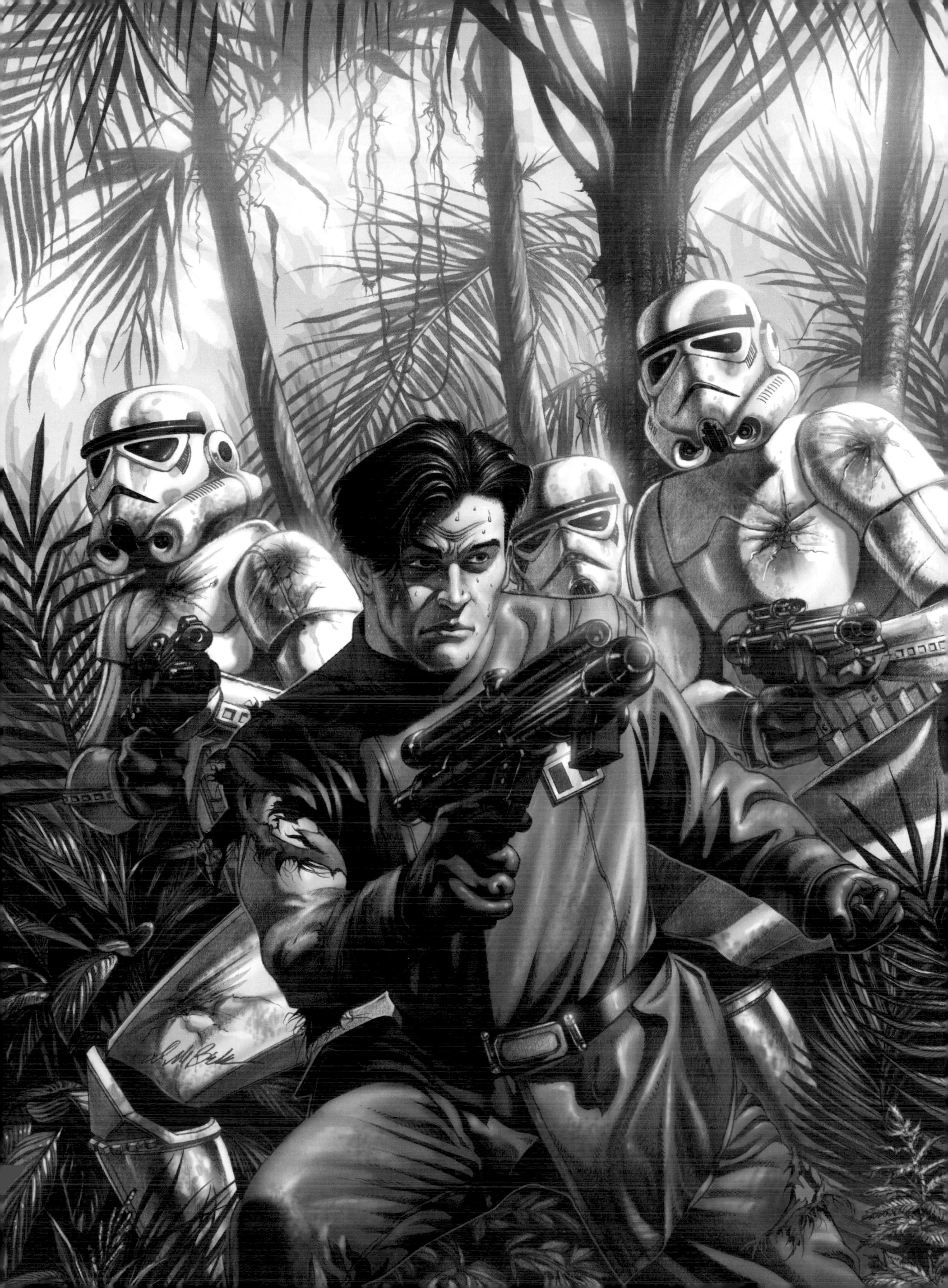

These two pages: art by Dave Dorman. Above: from the graphic story album Dark Forces: Jedi Knight *(1998). Facing page:* X-Wing: Rogue Squadron *#4 (1996).*

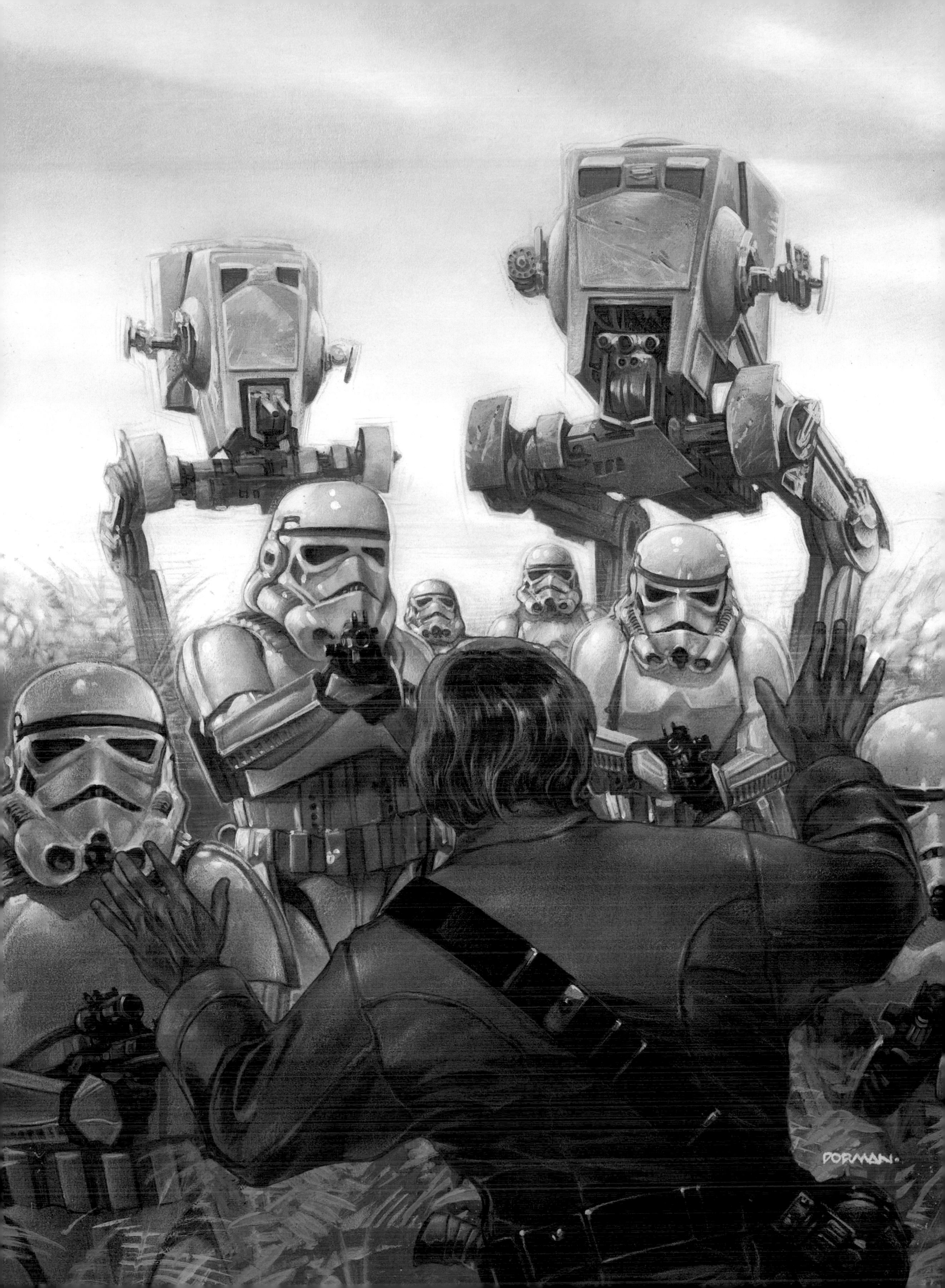
DORMAN

OTHER VILLAINS AND ROGUES

Ranking below (but only just) the Sith and the Imperials, was another class of villains, often unaffiliated with any government, movement, or ancient religion. Some of these villains were genuinely evil, while others were simply morally ambiguous enough to overlook the suffering of others if there was a profit to be made.

Asajj Ventress in her younger days. Adopted and trained by a Jedi Master who had crash-landed on her war-torn homeworld of Rattatak, Ventress was discovered by Count Dooku. He convinced her that the Jedi had abandoned her now-deceased Master and turned her to the dark side for his own use.

Art by Brian Ching, colored by Brad Anderson. Republic #60 (2003).

101

The instigator behind many plots, His Immenseness, Jabba the Hutt.

Art by Monty Sheldon. Jabba the Hutt: The Art of the Deal *(1998).*

Asajj Ventress in her younger days. Adopted and trained by a Jedi Master who had crash-landed on her war-torn homeworld of Rattatak, Ventress was discovered by Count Dooku. He convinced her that the Jedi had abandoned her now-deceased Master and turned her to the dark side for his own use.

Art by Brian Ching, colored by Brad Anderson. Republic #60 (2003).

101

As a dark® Jedi, Asajj became *Commander* Ventress, leading some of Dooku's droid armies against the forces of the Republic. Here she is seen alongside former bounty hunter turned Jedi-killer Durge.

Durge is talking about Jedi. That's Obi-Wan under his foot.

Script by Haden Blackman, pencils by Tomás Giorello, inks by Curtis Arnold, colored by Brad Anderson, lettering by Digital Chameleon. From Republic #51 (2003), *collected in* Clone Wars Volume 1 (2003).

The instigator behind many plots, His Immenseness, Jabba the Hutt.

Art by Monty Sheldon. Jabba the Hutt: The Art of the Deal *(1998).*

Art by Mark Harrison. Jabba the Hutt: The Hunger of Princess Nampi *(1995), collected in* Jabba the Hutt: The Art of the Deal.

Thief, sneak, provocateur, cheat, and galaxy-class liar, Vilmarh Grahrk (known to his friends and enemies alike as "Villie") worked, at one time or another, for everyone from Darth Sidious to the Jedi—but always with an eye toward double-crossing his employers. A rogue, but an endearing one, he always managed to escape with his skin intact.

When Villie encountered Quinlan Vos, a Jedi who had lost his memory, he delighted in manipulating what he liked to call his "pet Jedi." The fun lasted until Master Vos got his memory back.

The man who would be emperor. Carnor Jax was the best of Palpatine's elite Imperial Guards. Some seven years after the events in *Return of the Jedi*, Jax's greed for power—and the discovery of his own slight abilities with the Force—led him to betray his cloned master and his fellow guardsmen.

In his bid for control over the remnants of Palpatine's empire, Jax surrounded himself with specially trained, black-clad stormtroopers.

Carnor Jax's one mistake was allowing Kir Kanos—also an Imperial Guard—to survive the ambush that killed their fellows. Loyal to the memory of the dead Palpatine and the honor of the squad, Kanos made it his mission to destroy Jax… and any who stood with him.

This page and facing: art by Dave Dorman. Above: Crimson Empire #1 (1997). *Facing:* Crimson Empire #3 (1998).

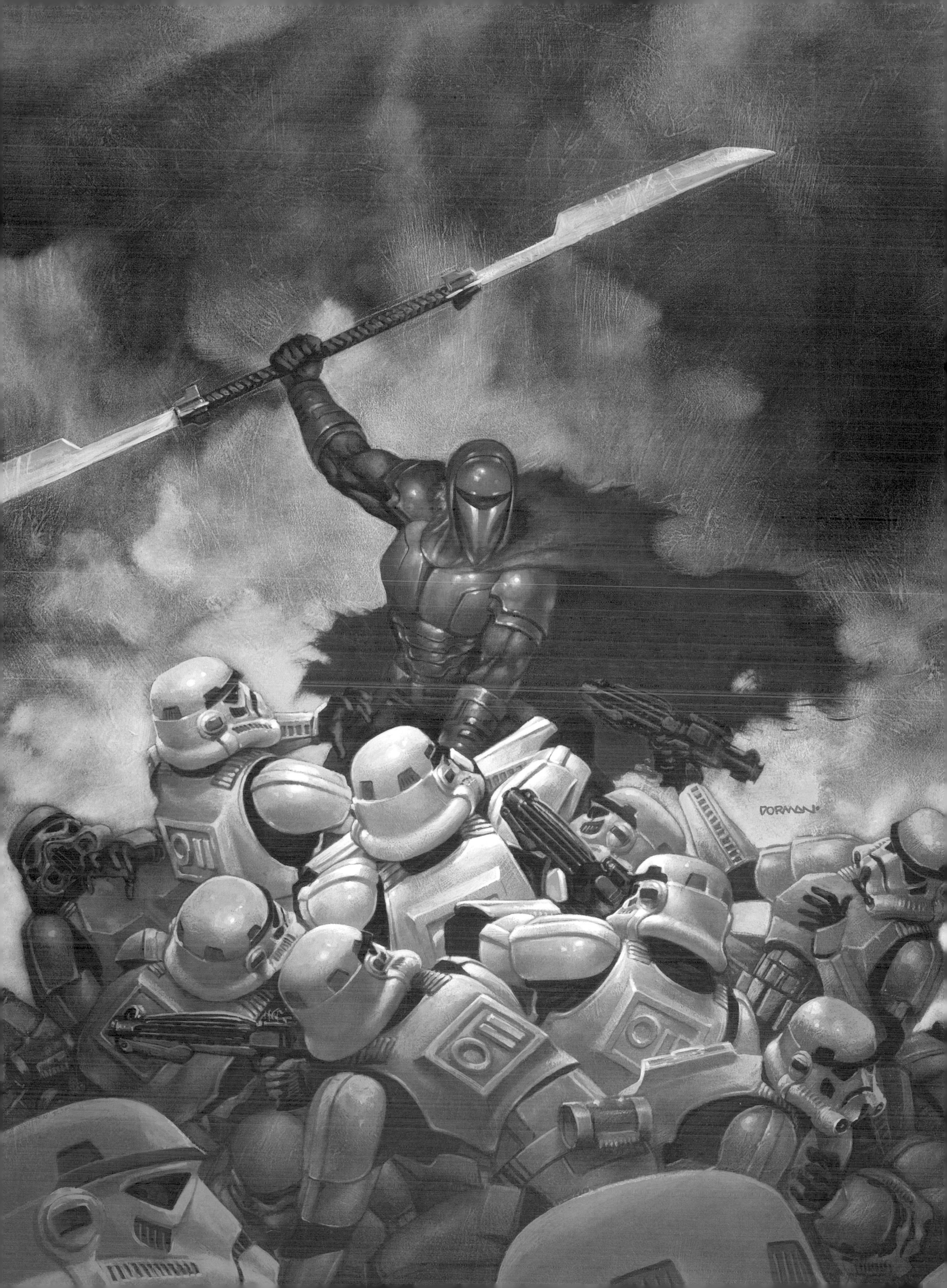
DORMAN

Though by this time both were deceased, the past actions of Palpatine and Vader informed the choices made by all of the players in *Crimson Empire*. (Note: that's not Jabba, it's Grappa, a major power in the criminal organization Black Sun.)

After Carnor Jax's short-lived reign had ended, an Imperial Interim Council—whose members had been secretly involved in Jax's plot against Palpatine—became the focus of Kir Kanos' vendetta. (Note: the character on the far left was modeled on Lucasfilm's own Lucy Wilson.)

Art by Dave Dorman. Crimson Empire II: Council of Blood #1 (1998).

113

BOUNTY HUNTERS

Some of the most famous characters in the *Star Wars* mythos are bounty hunters—men, women, and aliens living on the fringes of the law, and hunting their fellow sentients for a living.

With a bounty on his head for the assassination of Carnor Jax, former Imperial Guard Kir Kanos made a name for himself as bounty hunter Kenix Kil so that Kil would be hired to track down Kanos, thus assuring that he, Kanos, would never be found. Confused yet?

Art by Doug Wheatley, colored by Dave McCaig. Bounty Hunters: Kenix Kil *(1999).*

Once a Jedi Padawan herself, bounty hunter Aurra Sing's specialty was killing Jedi for fun and profit (she had quite a collection of trophy lightsabers). However, she was adept at dealing with other adversaries, as well.

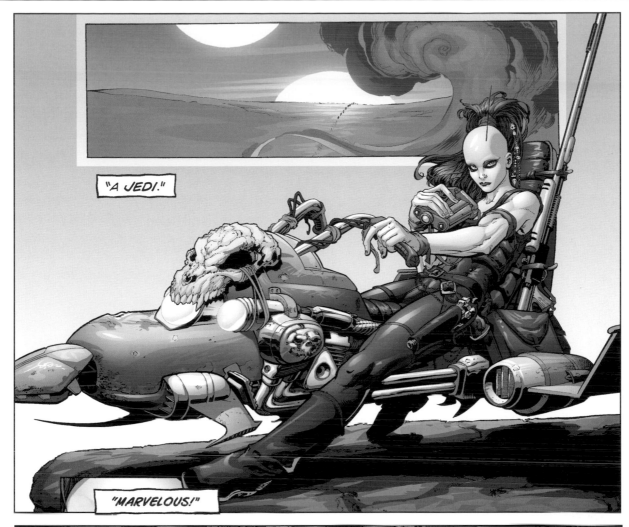

"A JEDI."

"MARVELOUS!"

Top: script by Tim Truman, pencils by Rob Pereira, inks by Mark Lipka, colored by Dave McCaig. From Star Wars #7 (1999). Collected in Outlander *(2001). Bottom: script by John Ostrander, pencils by Davidé Fabbri, inks by Christian Dalla Vecchia, colored by Dave McCaig. From* Star Wars #29 (2001), collected in The Hunt for Aurra Sing *(2002).*

Aurra's Jedi-hunting ways eventually landed her in prison—but never for very long. A resourceful survivor, for a while she even possessed Jango Fett's ship *Slave I*—after Jango lost his head in *Attack of the Clones*.

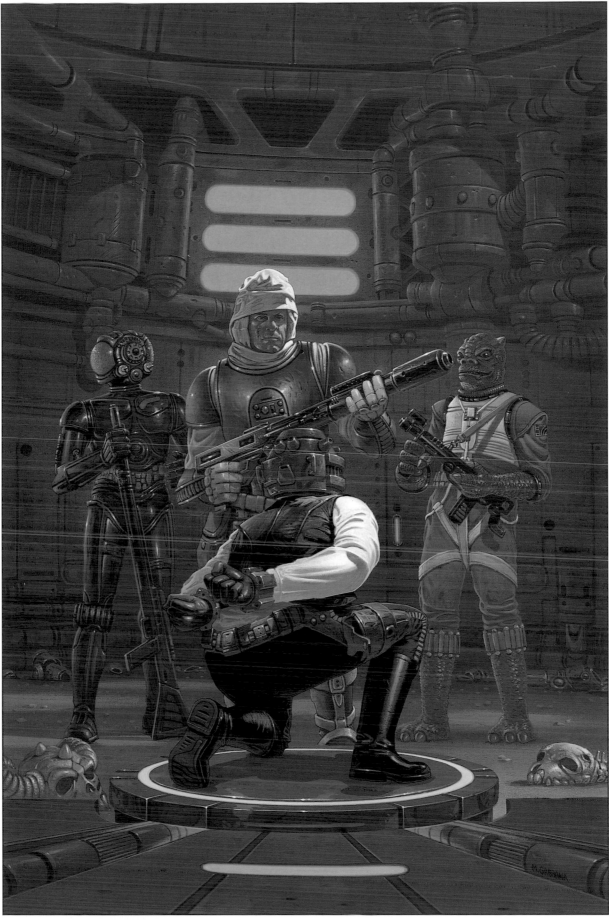

Made famous by their brief appearances in *The Empire Strikes Back*, bounty hunters 4-LOM (left), Dengar (center), and Bossk (right) were a continuing source of danger for the heroes of Yavin. The surprise here is that the guy wearing the handcuffs and the Corellian Bloodstripe trousers (Second Class) isn't Han Solo—it's Lando Calrissian.

Art by Marc Gabbana. Bounty Hunters: Scoundrel's Wages *(1999).*

While not technically bounty hunters, Jabba's henchmen Big Gizz and Spiker were willing to take on virtually any unscrupulous job, no questions asked.

Some bounty hunters lived longer than others because they knew that some bounties just weren't worth the risk...

Art by Brian Ching, colored by Brad Anderson. Republic #62 (2004).

121

Clockwise from lower left: 4-LOM, Dengar, Aurra Sing, Kenix Kil, Bossk, and the most famous bounty hunter in the galaxy, Boba Fett. Much was made of Fett's association with "Mandalorian Commandos" in the Expanded Universe before George Lucas revealed the truth of his origins in *Attack of the Clones*. Fans (and comic-book editors) are still trying to sort it out.

Art by Dave Dorman. Bounty Hunters *(2000). Facing page: art by Tsuneo Sanda. The cover to* Star Wars Tales *Volume 2 (2001).*

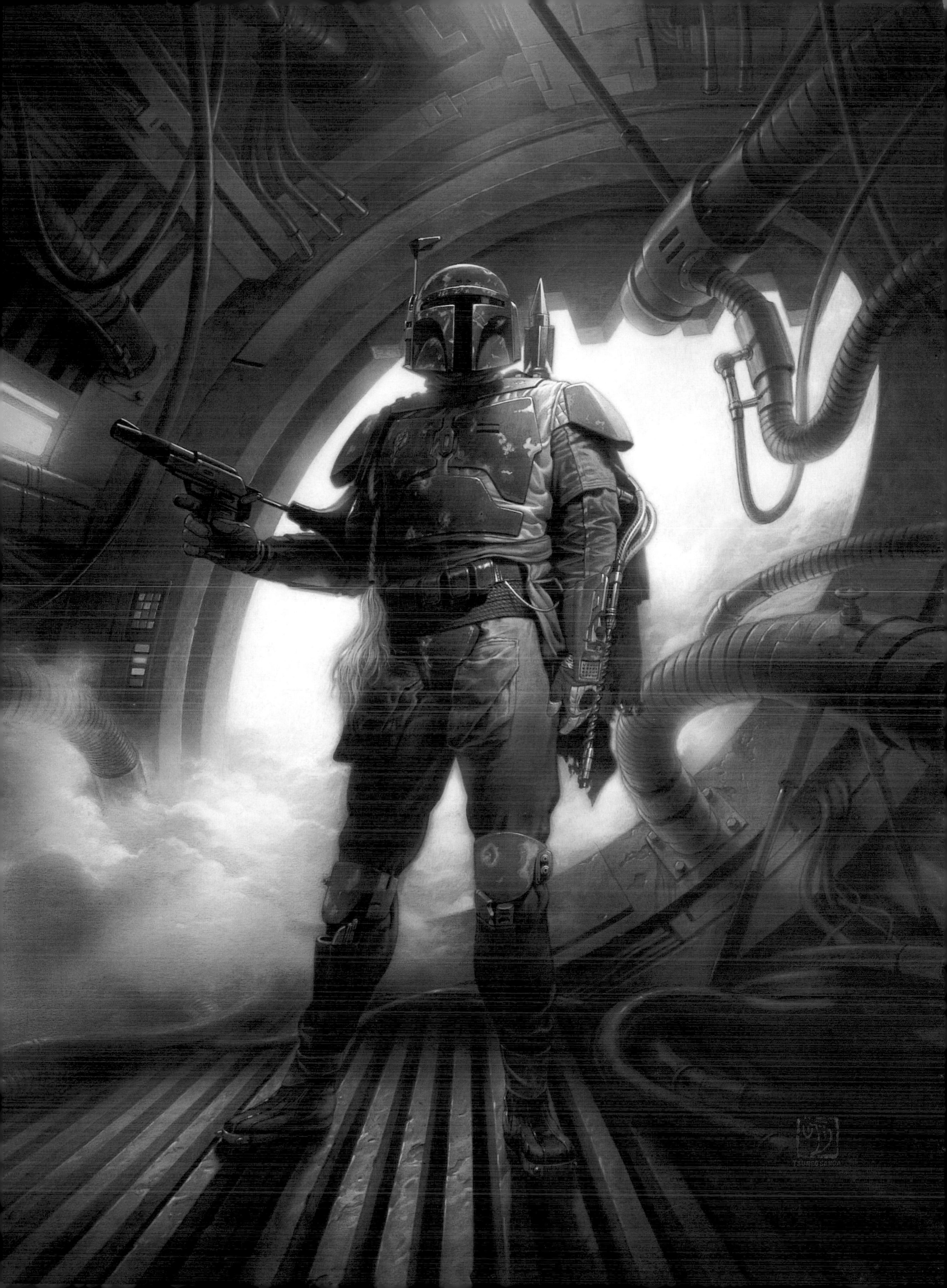

Though he had only a couple of lines in *The Empire Strikes Back*, and was done away with in the first twenty minutes of *Return of the Jedi*, fan interest in the mysterious, helmeted bounty hunter continued to run high. Eventually it was learned that Fett clawed his way out of the Sarlacc pit into which he'd fallen and returned to strike fear into the hearts of those with a price on their heads.

Script by Beau Smith, pencils by Mike Deodato, Jr., inks by Neil Nelson, coloring by Dave McCaig, lettering by Steve Dutro. From the story "Outbid But Never Outgunned" in Star Wars Tales #7 (2001), *collected in* Tales Volume 2 (2002).

Fett did his share of work for the Empire, but he was a free agent, and was occasionally hired for jobs that put him at odds with the powers that be.

Art by Ken Kelly. Boba Fett: Enemy of the Empire #1 *(1999), collected in the graphic novel of the same name (1999).*

Art by Dave Dorman. Dark Empire II *#2 (1995).*

While Boba, Jango's clone, became famous—and feared—throughout the galaxy, Jango Fett's most important legacy was without a doubt his contribution to the creation of the clone army first seen in *Attack of the Clones*.

THE JEDI

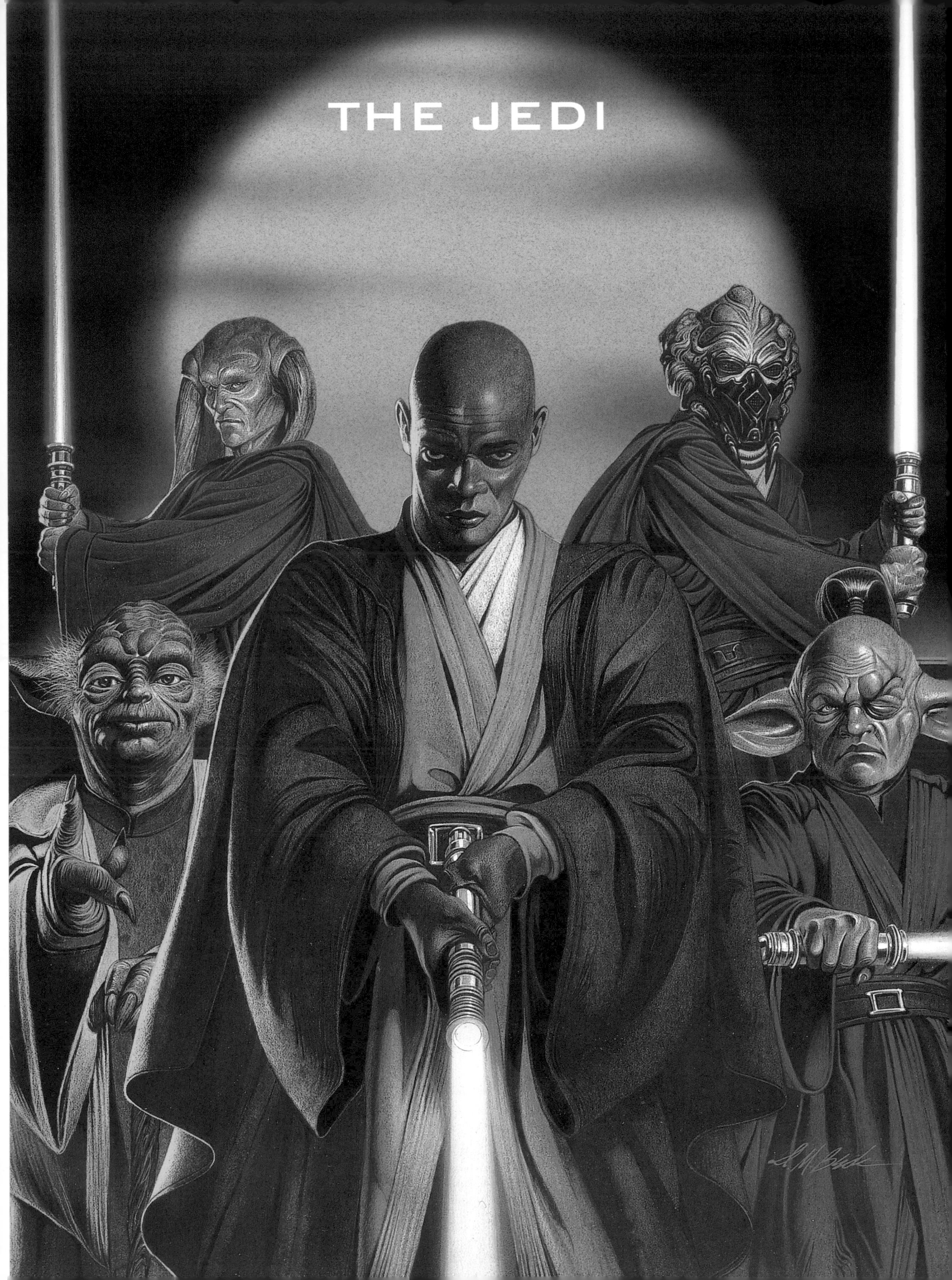

THE PROTECTORS OF THE REPUBLIC

For a thousand generations, they were the champions of the Old Republic. Though their origins are shrouded in the dimness of time, and the details of their fall are yet to be revealed, there is not a kid (or an adult) who has seen the *Star Wars* films who hasn't wished to be a Jedi. More than mystic do-gooders in robes, the Jedi were akin to samurai monks. Calm in the face of adversity but ready for any danger, every Jedi was equipped with mysterious Force powers and the best invention in science fiction and fantasy, bar none—a lightsaber.

Previous page: art by David Michael Beck. Jedi Council: Acts of War (2001).

Though cut short by Darth Maul's lightsaber, Qui-Gon Jinn's life was not in vain. The lessons he taught his Padawan, Obi-Wan Kenobi, became central to the destruction of the Empire and the redemption of Anakin Skywalker. **Next page:** The leader of the Jedi Council during the Clone Wars, Mace Windu embodied the ideal combination of reasoned cool and decisive, lightning-fast action.

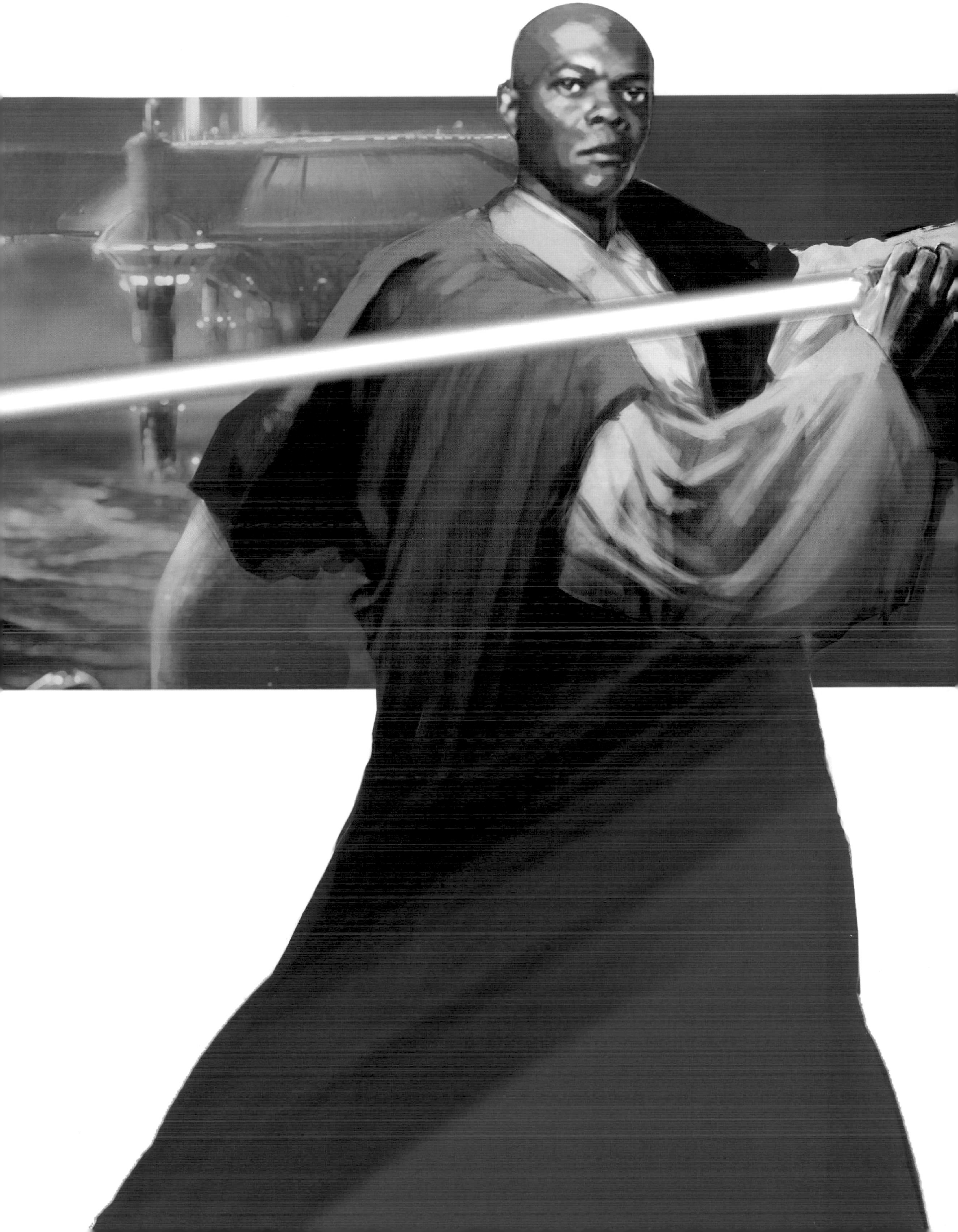

Jedi came in all shapes and sizes—and were recruited from nearly every sentient species in the galaxy. On this spread we have Wookiee Master Tyvokka and Master A'Sharad Hett. Hett lived with the Tusken Raiders (though he himself was human), and adopted many of their ways. After the events in *Attack of the Clones*, his relationship with Anakin Skywalker was somewhat strained.

This page: art by Jan Duursema, colored by Dave McCaig. Star Wars #37 (2001), *collected in* The Stark Hyperspace War *(2003). Next page: art by Ken Kelly.* Star Wars #10 (1999), *collected in* Outlander *(2001).*

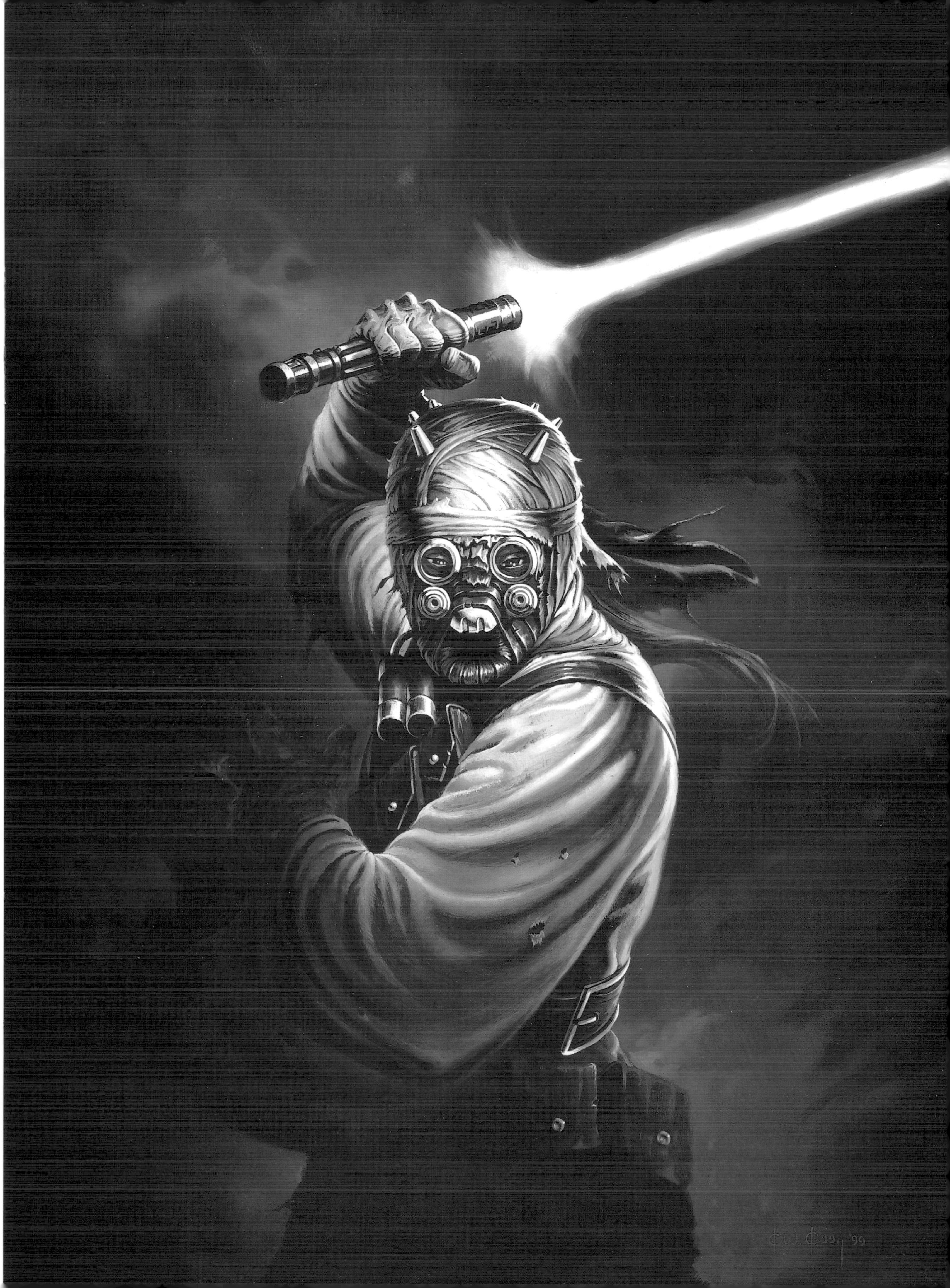

"A Jedi shall not know love." But apparently nobody said anything about making out… Above, Aayla Secura receives an assist from fellow-Jedi Kit Fisto. Below, Jedi-gone-bad Quinlan Vos and his uh, er, friend Khaleen Hentz.

Top: script by Dave Land, pencils by Adriana Melo, inks by Fabio Laguna, colored by Chris Blythe, lettering by Steve Dutro. From "Tides of Terror" in Star Wars Tales *#14 (2003), collected in* Tales Volume 4 *(2004). Bottom: script by John Ostrander, art by Jan Duursema, colored by Brad Anderson. From* Jedi: Count Dooku *(2003), collected in* Clone Wars Volume 4 *(2004).*

Aayla Secura again. George Lucas liked the look of Aayla so much that he inserted her into *Attack of the Clones*. It's a good thing creative team John Ostrander and Jan Duursema didn't kill her off as they had originally planned...

The Jedi legacy lives on. Some eight years after the events in *Return of the Jedi*, Luke Skywalker's pupils face a do or die challenge. If they survive, they will have proved themselves worthy of the title Jedi.

Art by David Michael Beck. The graphic novel Jedi Academy: Leviathan *(2000).*

SPACESHIPS

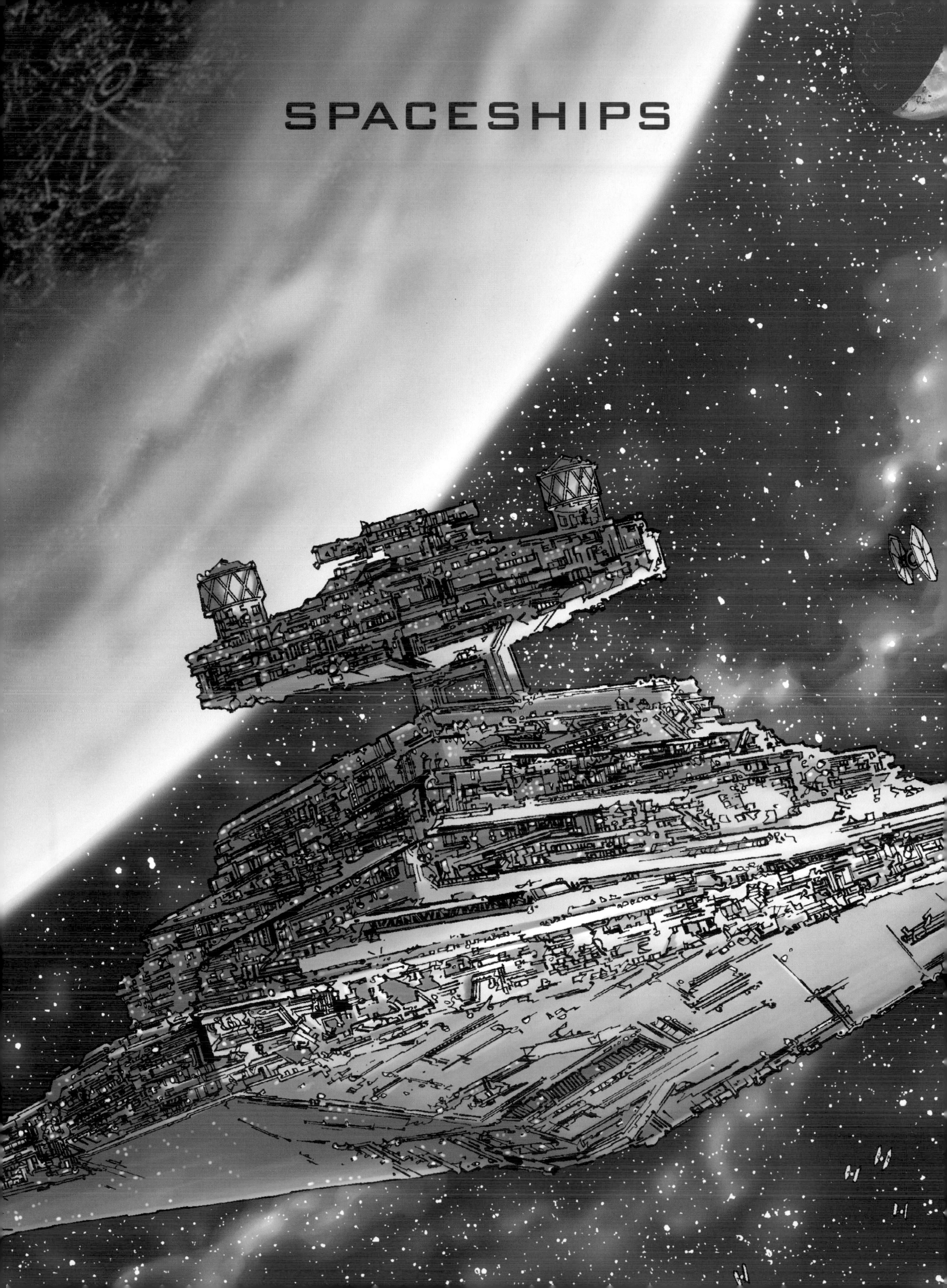

GETTING AROUND THE GALAXY

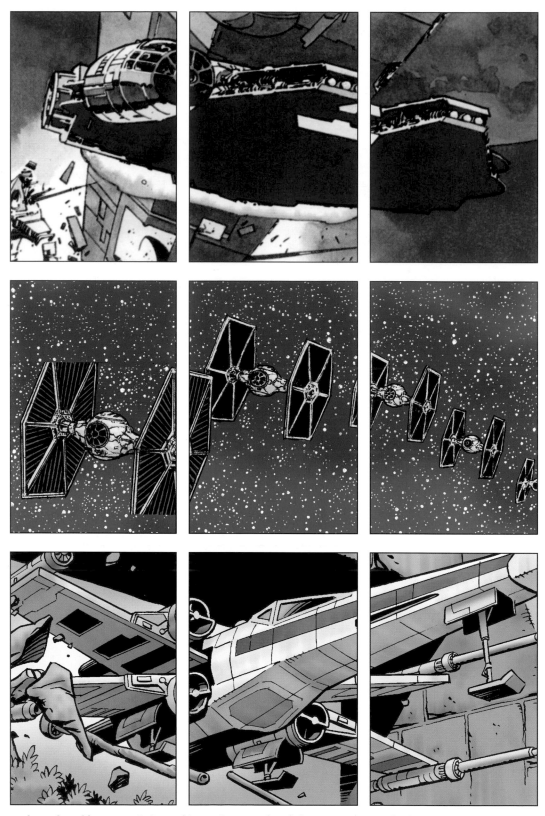

In the real world, even a trip into orbit requires months of planning. Fortunately, thanks to astromech droids and hyperspace travel, in *Star Wars* getting from one end of the galaxy is no more trouble than hopping in one's car for a drive across town. From the gigantic Imperial Star Destroyers to the tiny Rebel snub fighters, the spacecraft in *Star Wars* serve not only as story conveniences, but as potent fuel for the imaginations of the viewers and readers.

Previous page: pencils by Ryan Benjamin, inks by Curtis Arnold, colored by Dave Stewart. From Empire #1 *(2002), collected in* Empire Volume 1 *(2003).*

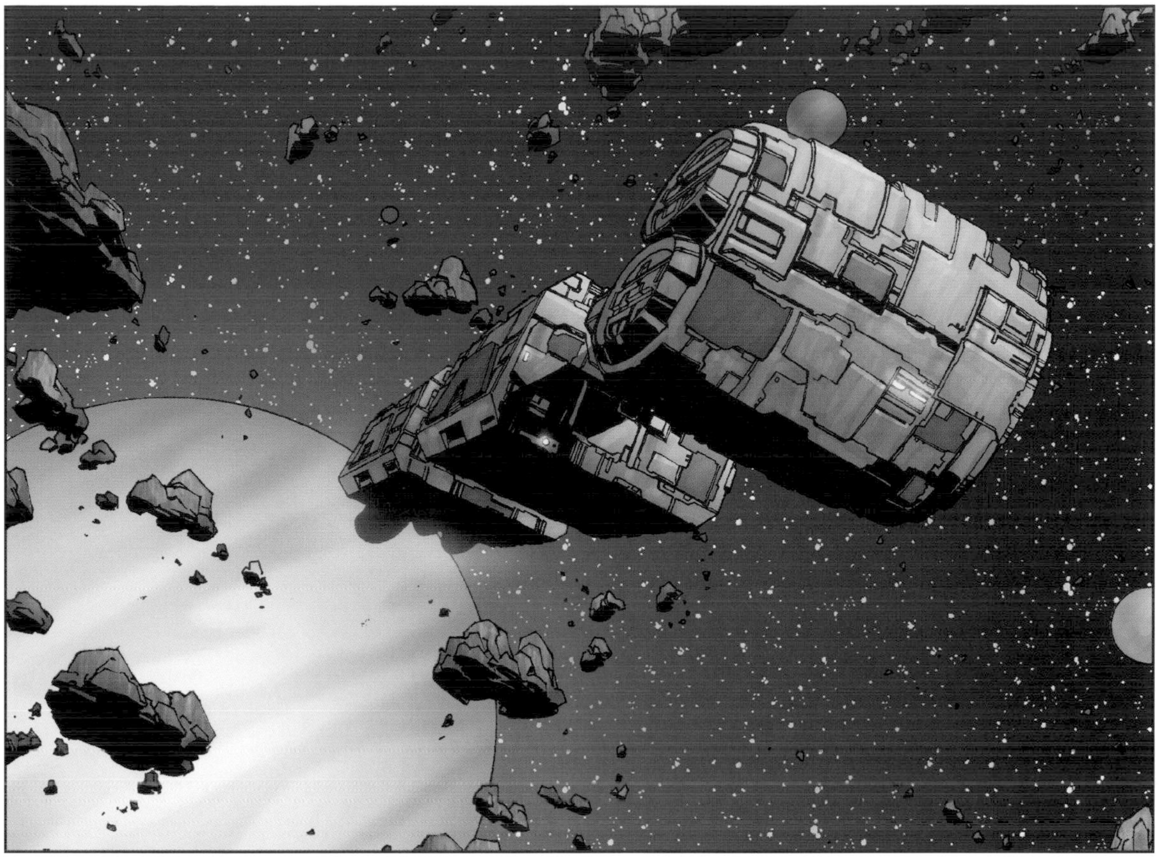

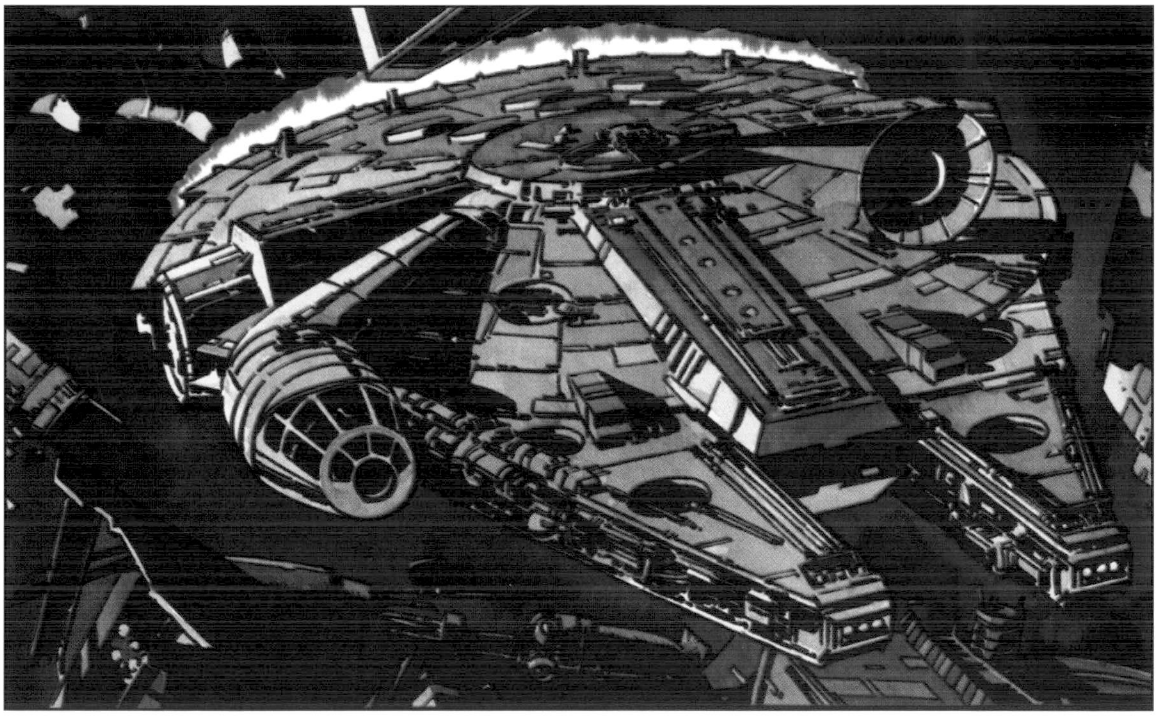

Top: Art by Pop Mhan, colored by Dave Nestelle. From the Star Wars Handbook *#3:* Dark Empire *(1999). Bottom: art by Cam Kennedy, from* Dark Empire *#1 (1992), collected in* Dark Empire *(1993).*

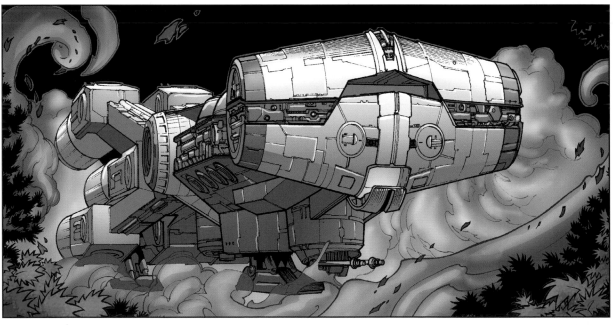

Not enough credit has been given to the designers involved in *Star Wars*. Even the spacecraft have personality. Those serving the side of good and freedom reflect a human esthetic in their lines and their color schemes…

Top: script by Mike Baron, pencils by Olivier Vatine, inks by Fred Blanchard, colored by Isabelle Rabarot, lettering by Ellie DeVille. From Heir to the Empire *(1996).*
Bottom: pencils by Davidé Fabbri, inks by Christian Dalla Vecchia, colored by Brad Anderson. From Empire #6 *(2003).*

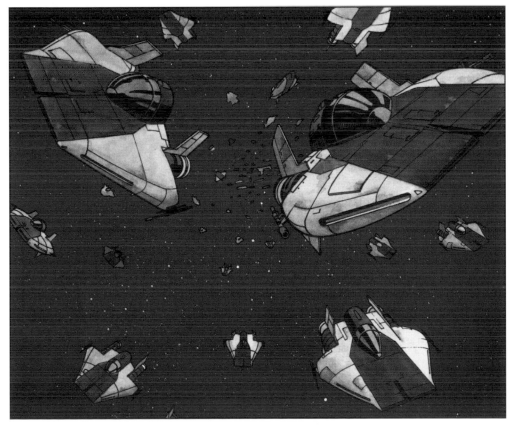

Bottom: pencils by Terry Dodson, inks by Kevin Nowlan, colored by Pamela Rambo. From Dark Force Rising *(1996).*

...while those built for the Empire are cold and machine-like, with little concern for human need or comfort.

These two pages: art by Dean Williams. From the graphic story album Dark Forces: Soldier for the Empire *(1997).*

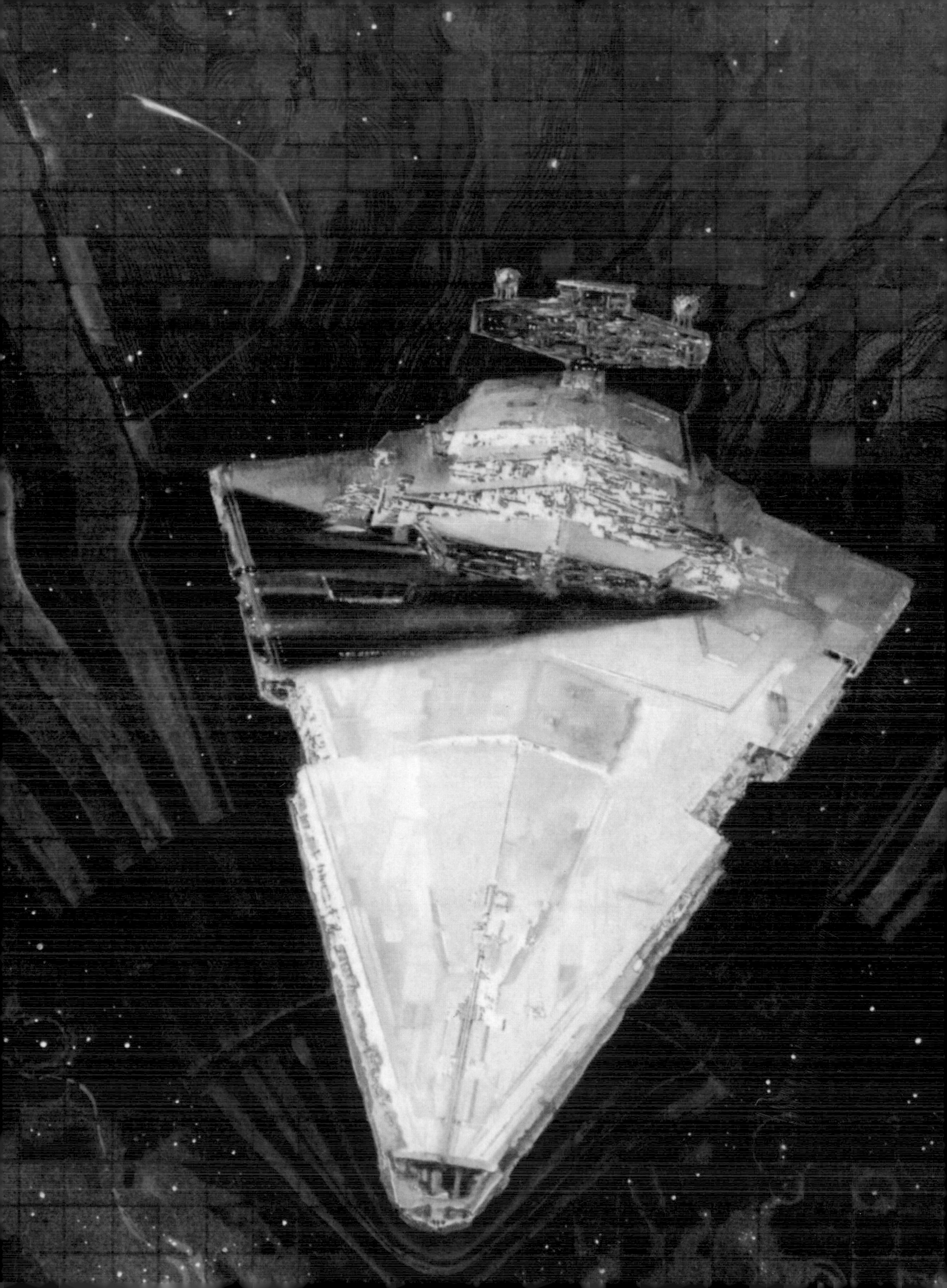

After Vader's breathing and the electrifying hum of a lightsaber's ignition, one of the most recognizable sounds in cinema history is the hoarse scream of an Imperial TIE fighter in pursuit of its prey. And who can forget the awe of seeing for the first time the endless hull of a Star Destroyer slide by in the opening sequence of *A New Hope?* **Facing page:** Rogue Squadron on patrol for the Rebel Alliance.

This page: script by Mike Baron, pencils by Olivier Vatine, inks by Fred Blanchard, colored by Isabelle Rabarot, lettering by Ellie DeVille. From Heir to the Empire #3 *(1995), collected 1996. Facing page: script by Mike Stackpole and Jan Strnad, art by Gary Erskine, colored by Dave Nestelle, lettering by Annie Parkhouse. From* X-Wing: Rogue Squadron #19 *(1997), collected in* Requiem for a Rogue *(1999).*

OKAY, WEDGE-- SPILL IT! THIS SCOUTING MISSION IS JUST AN EXCUSE TO GET AWAY FROM PRYING BOTHAN EARS, RIGHT?
YES AND NO, TYCHO. IS YOUR COMM UNIT LOCKED IN AND SCRAMBLED, WES?
I'M PLUGGED IN, WEDGE!

Once planetside, there were other methods of transportation available, but an Imperial speeder bike might not be your first choice…

Art by Dave Dorman. From the graphic story album Dark Forces: Jedi Knight *(1998).*

Script by Tom Veitch, art by Cam Kennedy, lettering by Todd Klein. From Dark Empire *(1993).*

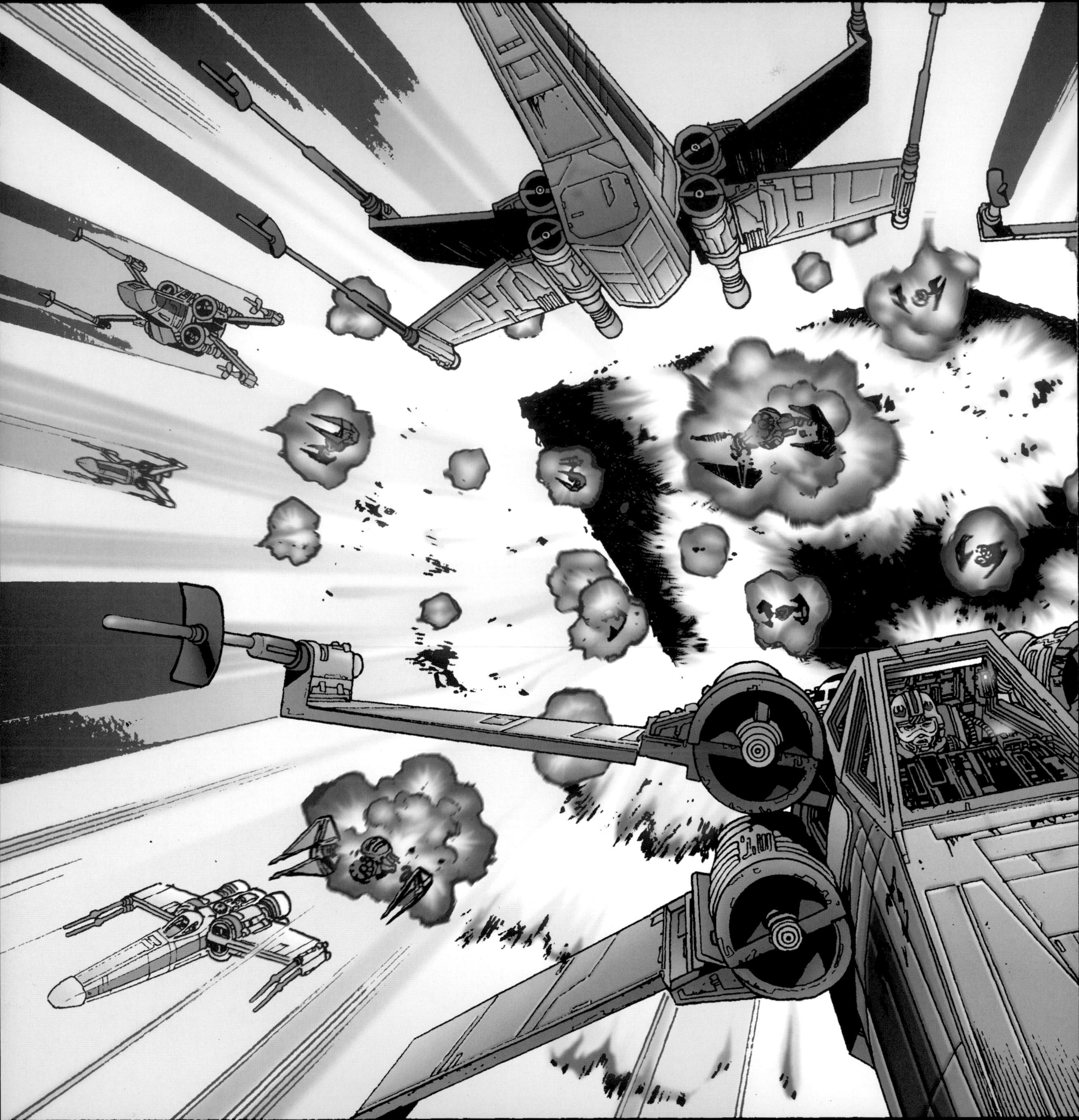

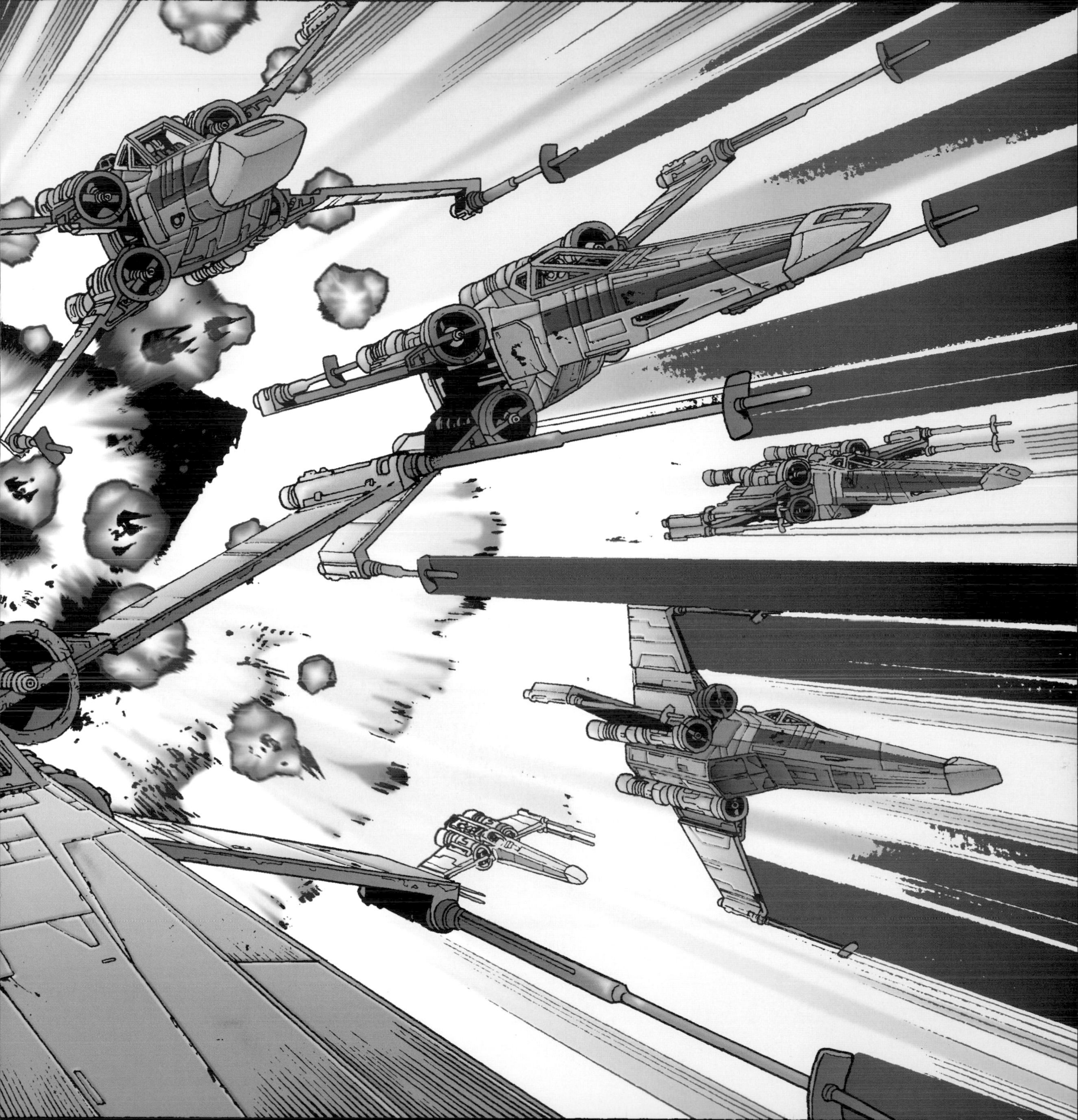

While the X-wing fighter is the most familiar of the craft used by the Rebel Alliance, as the war against the Empire progressed, new fighters were commissioned. These A-wings (first seen in *Return of the Jedi*) here are engaged in a funeral procession. Being a Rebel meant putting one's life on the line on a daily basis.

A not uncommon sight: Boba Fett in *Slave I* pursuing Han Solo and Chewbacca in the *Millennium Falcon*.

Expanded Universe sources suggest that the open cage structures behind the Y-wing's engines were originally sheathed in plating—that mechanics quickly discarded in order to provide easier maintenance. Considered obsolete at the time of the Battle of Yavin, the solidly built Y-wing nonetheless served double duty as fighters and fighter-bombers for a number of years to come.

But it was the doughty X-wing that carried the day in *both* battles against Imperial Death Stars.

Art by John Nadeau. X-Wing: Rogue Squadron *#22 (1997), collected in* In the Empire's Service *(1999).*

A recurring: theme in *Star Wars*: no matter where you're going, it seems somebody is always trying to prevent you from getting there. In this case, a Republic gunship, circa the Clone Wars, is pursued by Trade Federation droid fighters.

Script by Jason Hall, pencils by Francis Portela, inks by Albert Xiques, coloring and lettering by Digital Chameleon. From "Machines of War," a comics premium produced for Hasbro and Toys "R" Us (2002).

THE WORLDS OF *STAR WARS*

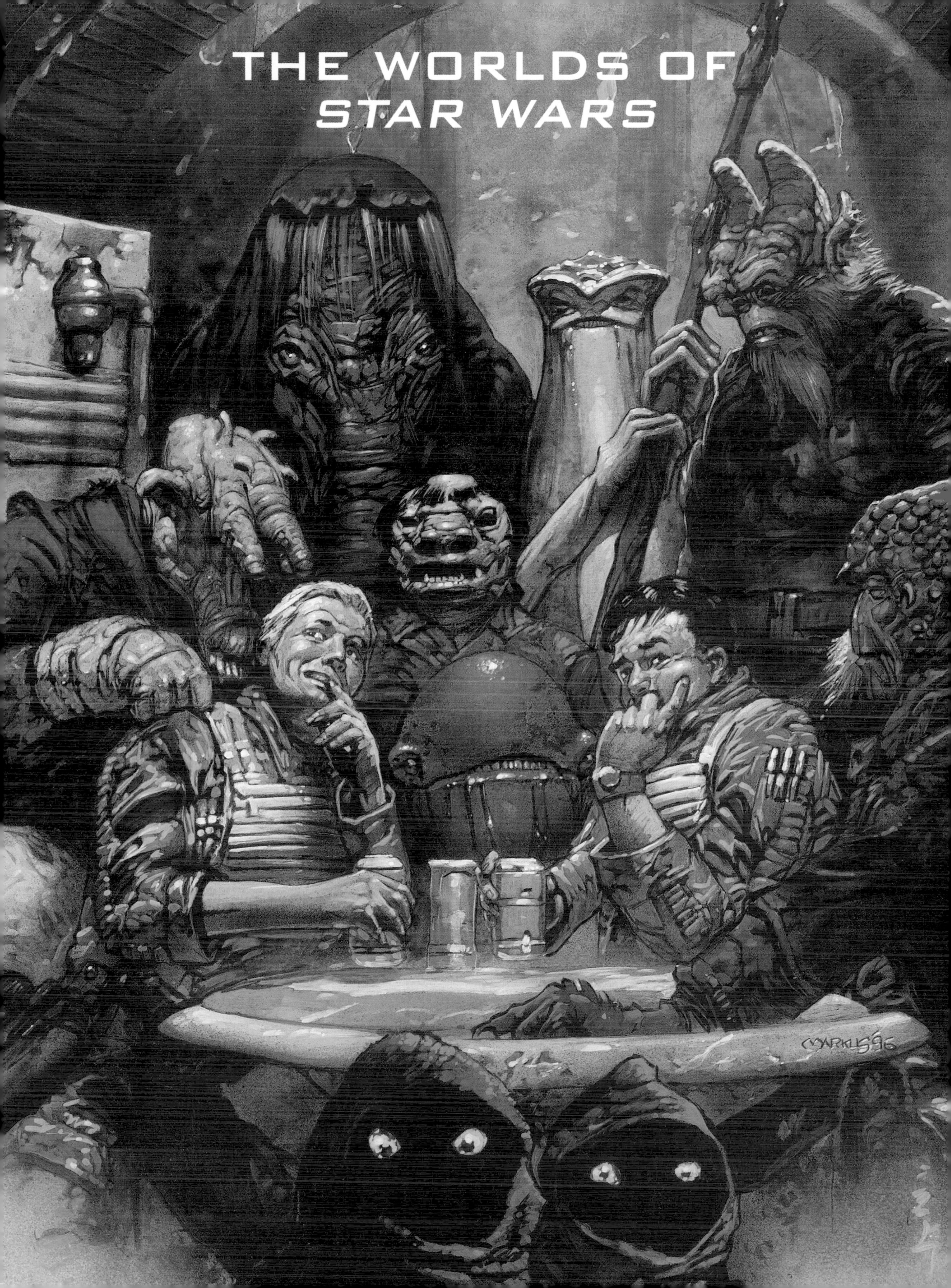
MARKUS'96

ALIEN WORLDS AND THEIR INHABITANTS

Frightening, amusing, or wonderful, the many alien species that populate the galaxy are an undeniable component of *Star Wars'* allure. For what would an exotic new world be without exotic new creatures—some friendly (or at least approachable), and some deadly dangerous? Ancient civilizations, bizarre technologies, and fantastic flora and fauna are to be expected with each new locale. And there's no doubt we have been shown but the tip of the iceberg; at the height of the Republic, its members hailed from over one hundred thousand planetary systems!

Previous page: art by Mark Harrison. X-Wing: Rogue Squadron #9 (1996).

There was a single, vaguely threatening Amanin (sometimes referred to as Amanaman) lurking among Jabba the Hutt's cronies in *Return of the Jedi*. These unfortunate stormtroopers have discovered what the jungle-dwelling aliens are like when they get together in a group.

Wherever you go in the *Star Wars* galaxy, you know *where* you are. Tatooine doesn't look like Naboo, Abregado-Rae (top) doesn't look like Ossus (bottom), and there's no place in the universe like Coruscant (opposite).

168   *This page, top: script by Mike Baron, pencils by Olivier Vatine, inks by Fred Blanchard, colored by Isabelle Rabarot, lettering by Ellie DeVille. From* Heir to the Empire #4 *(1995), collected 1996. Bottom: script by Tom Veitch, art by Cam Kennedy, lettering by Todd Klein. From* Dark Empire II #3 *(1994), collected 1995.*

CORUSCANT--CAPITAL PLANET OF THE REPUBLIC.

Above: script by Tim Truman, pencils by Davidé Fabbri, inks by Christian Dalla Vecchia, colored by Dave McCaig, lettering by Steve Dutro. From Star Wars #28 (2001), *collected in* The Hunt for Aurra Sing *(2002).*

At its core, *Star Wars* is about the struggle between good and evil, light and darkness, and between freedom and tyranny. It is a struggle played out across thousands of years, on countless worlds. Only battles are won, never the war. The spirit of freedom faces never-ending challenges.

This page: art by Hugh Fleming. Tales of the Jedi: Dark Lords of the Sith *#2 (1994), collected in 1996. Facing page: art by Dave Dorman. From* Dark Forces: Jedi Knight *(1999).*

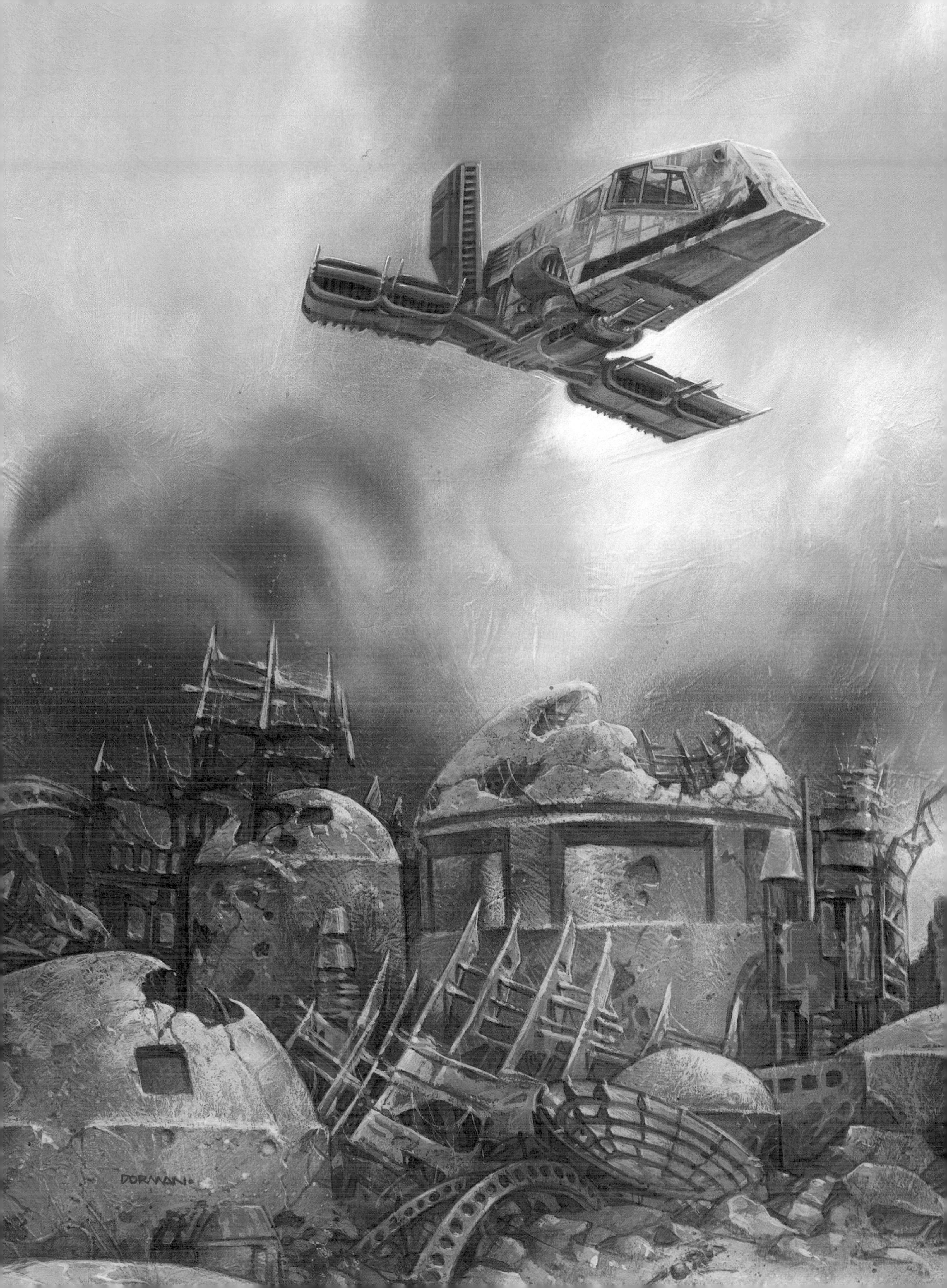
DORMAN

Even when it's a battle against the elements, it's rarely about simple survival. Instead, it's about helping a friend—or an old paramour—even at the risk of one's own life.

Script by Ron Marz, art by Tomás Giorello, colored by Michael Atiyeh, lettering by Michael David Thomas. From Empire *#20 (2004).*

And sometimes it *is* just about survival—as one species fights another for its place in the sun...

...or its corner of the ocean...

Art by Mark Schultz, colored by Matthew Hollingsworth. Classic Star Wars #8 (1993).

...or *your* spot in *its* belly.

Art by Andrew Robinson, colored by Matthew Hollingsworth. Star Wars #24 (2000).

175

Throughout the *Star Wars* timeline, the contrast of the familiar with the alien provides a continuous backdrop of romance, adventure, danger, and mystery.

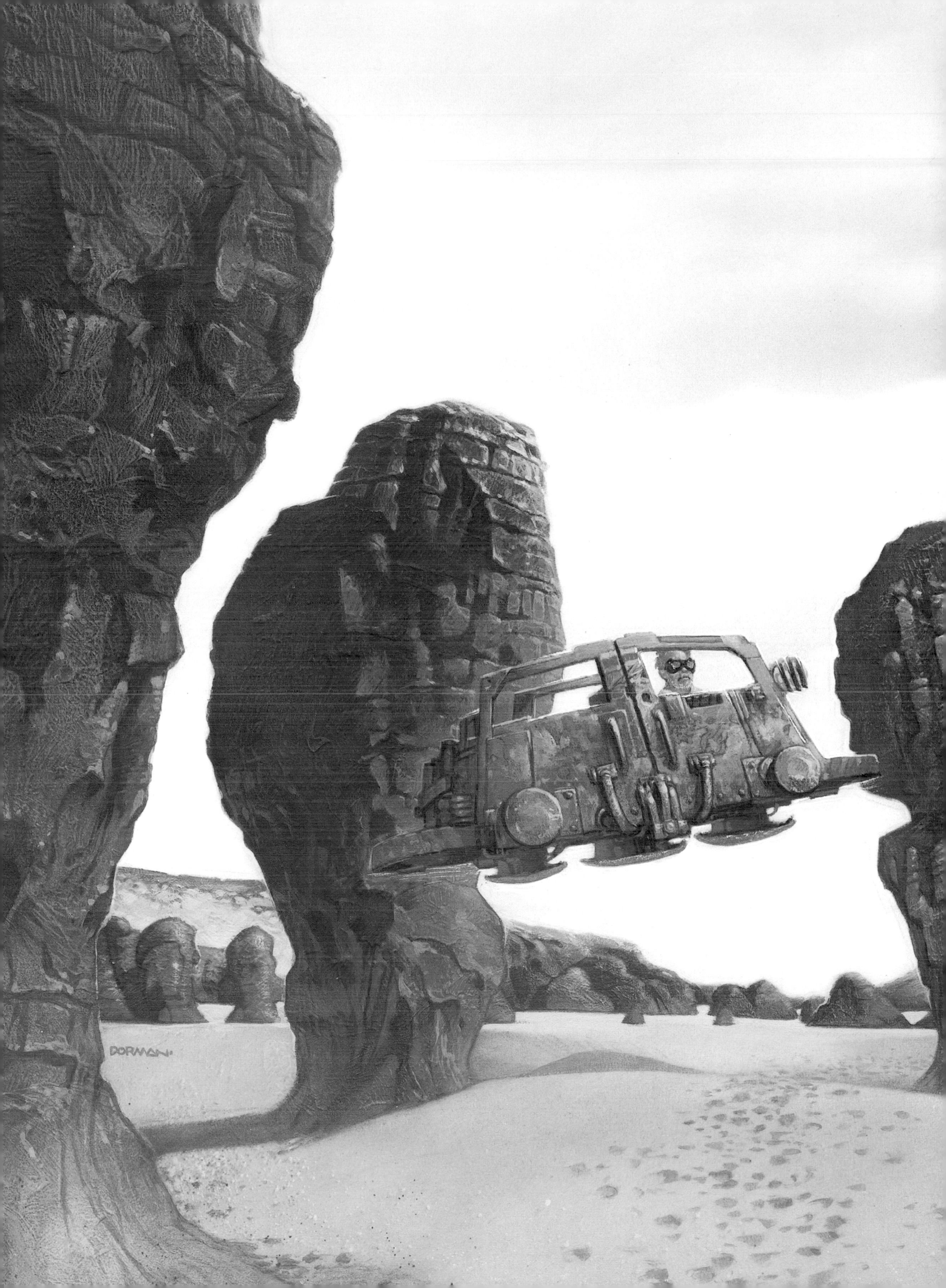
DORMAN

Top: pencils by Davidé Fabbri, inks by Christian Dalla Vecchia, colored by Dave McCaig. Jedi Council: Acts of War (2001). Center: art by Cary Nord, colored by Udon Entertainment. "Ghosts of Hoth," Star Wars Tales Volume 5 (2004). Bottom: art by Kellie Strom. "Fortune, Fate, and the Natural History of the Sarlacc," Star Wars Tales #6 (2000), collected in Star Wars Tales Volume 2 (2002). Opposite: art by Doug Wheatley, colored by Chris Chuckry. Empire Volume 2 (2004).

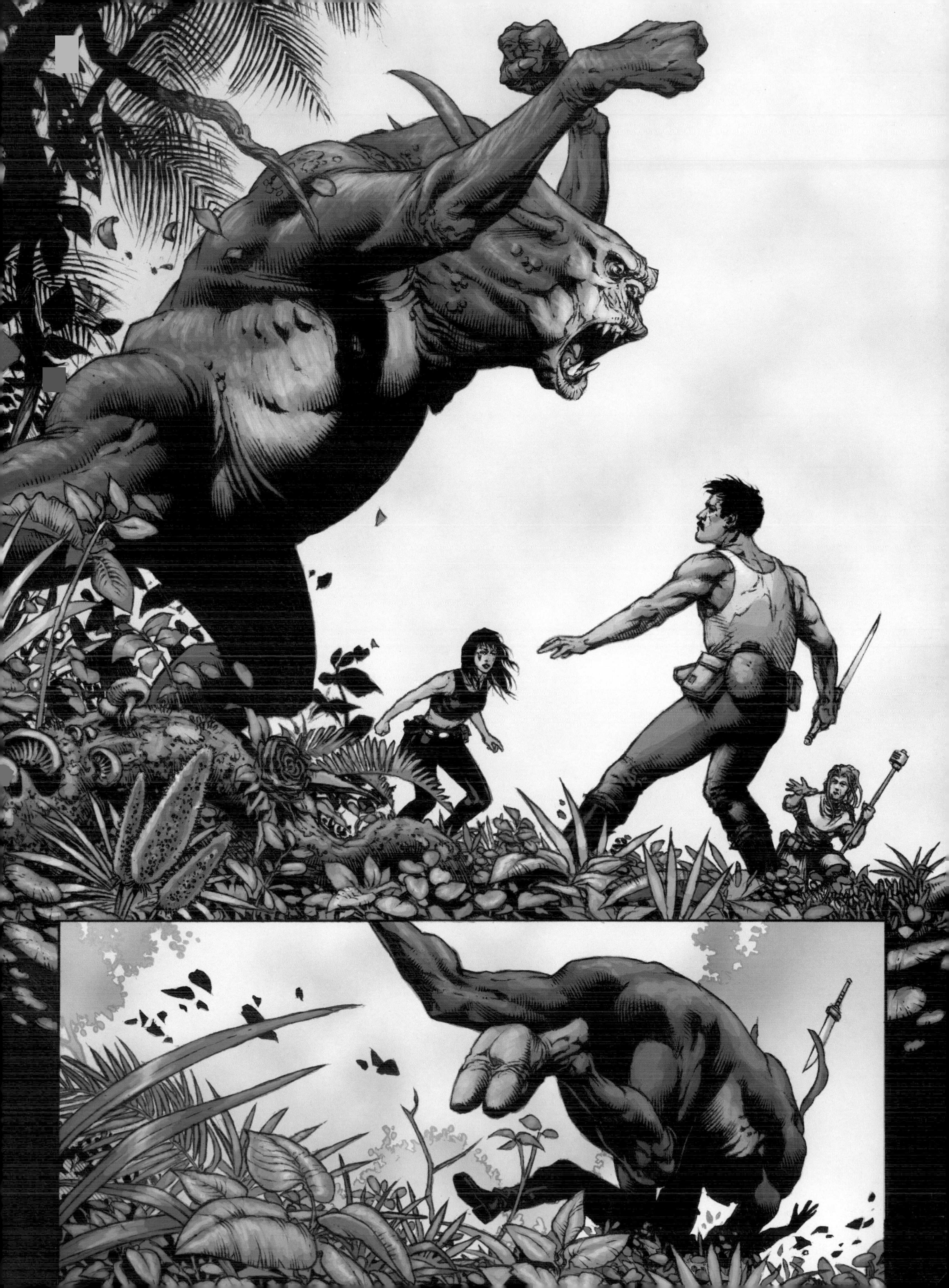

Top: script and art by Tim Truman, colored by Dave McCaig. Bounty Hunters: Aurra Sing *(1999), collected in* Bounty Hunters *(2000). Bottom: script by Tom Veitch, art by Cam Kennedy.* Dark Empire *(1994).*

And let us not forget—along with all of the organic life-forms in the galaxy, there exists a mechanical contingent: the droids. Some are nearly human in their behavior, while others are purely cold and functional—sometimes to a menacing degree. Note: a combat knife is not among the tools recommended for probe droid maintenance.

Art by Dave Dorman. Dark Forces: Jedi Knight *(1999).*

Even the meekest droid can become a force to be reckoned with given the right impetus, as Artoo and Threepio proved when they led a "rebellion" against a criminal intent on wiping the memories of a barge full of stolen droids.

Art by Kilian Plunkett. Droids: Rebellion *(1997).*

All hail…Threepio? As with all glory, this moment was fleeting.

Art by Kilian Plunkett, Droids #3 (1995).

From the inorganic to the super-organic: Chewbacca's homecoming. Think Wookiees are big? Check out the trees on their homeworld of Kashyyyk (the third "y" is silent).

Script by Mike Baron, pencils by Olivier Vatine, inks by Fred Blanchard, colored by Isabelle Rabarot, lettering by Ellie DeVille. From Heir to the Empire *(1996).*

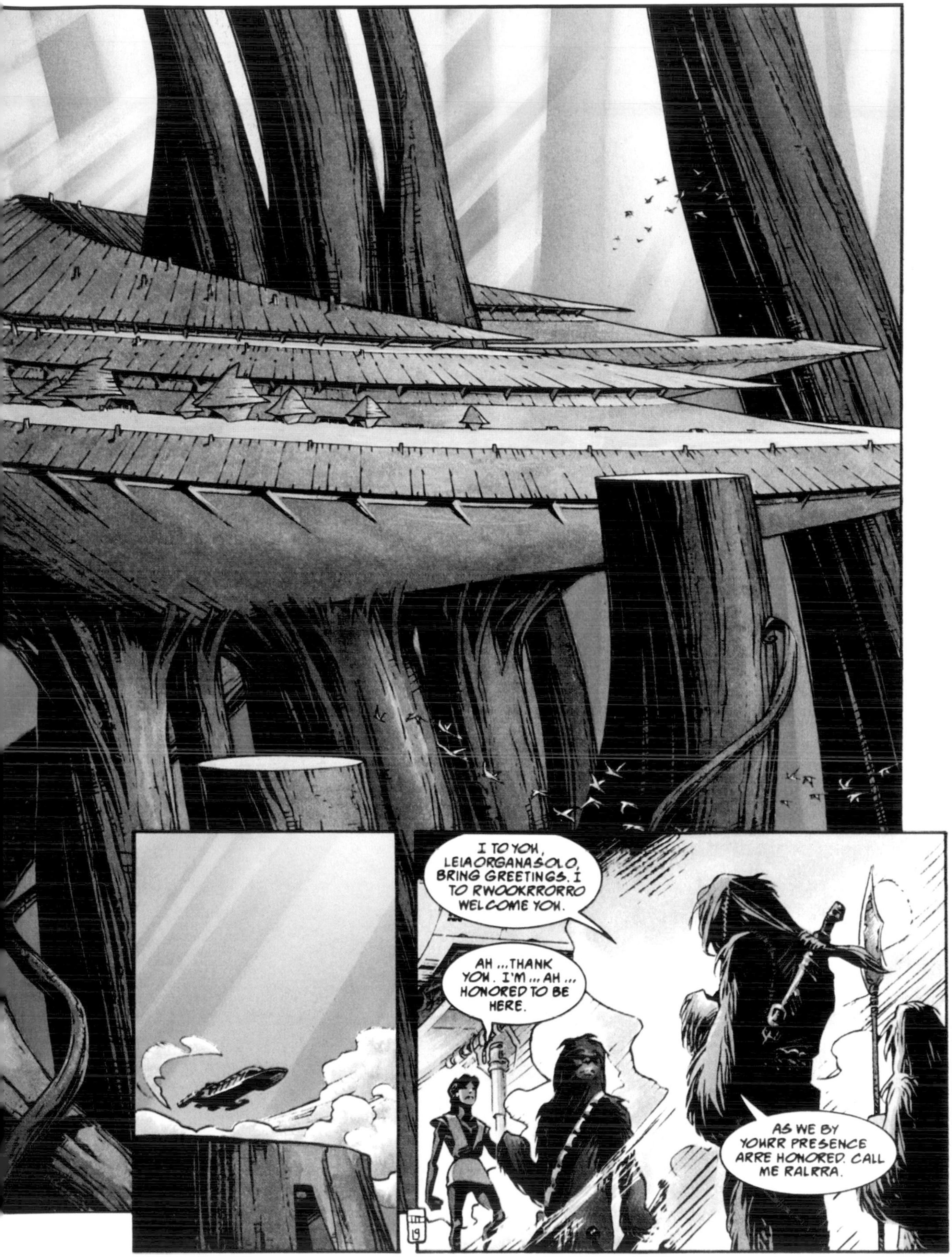
I TO YOU, LEIA ORGANA SOLO, BRING GREETINGS. I TO RWOOKRRORRO WELCOME YOU.
AH ... THANK YOU. I'M ... AH ... HONORED TO BE HERE.
AS WE BY YOURR PRESENCE ARRE HONORED. CALL ME RALRRA.

But mechanical or biological—or anywhere in-between—good and evil are forever at odds with one another in the *Star Wars* galaxy. That's the way it was at the birth of the Old Republic, and it will remain so even after the last glimmer of memory of the New Republic fades. Which means we can look forward to new adventures for years to come…

This page: art by Mark Harrison. X-Wing: Rogue Squadron #10 *(1996). Facing page: script by Tom Veitch, art by Cam Kennedy, lettering by Todd Klein.* Dark Empire *(1993). Page 188: art by Mark Harrison.* X-Wing: Rogue Squadron Special *(1996), a premium produced for Kellogg's* Apple Jacks *cereal, reprinted in* X-Wing: Rogue Squadron—Battleground: Tatooine *(1996).*

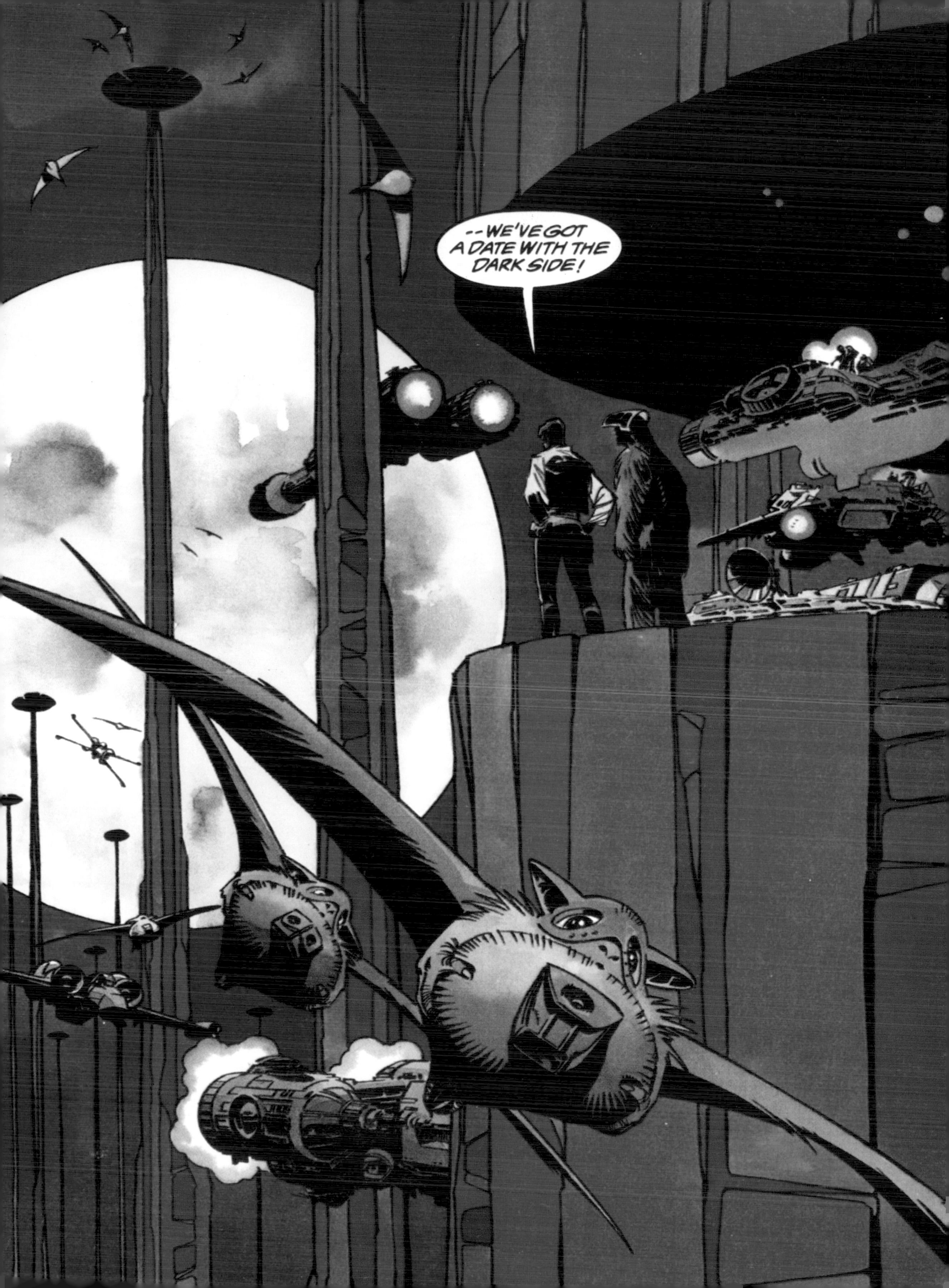
--WE'VE GOT A DATE WITH THE DARK SIDE!

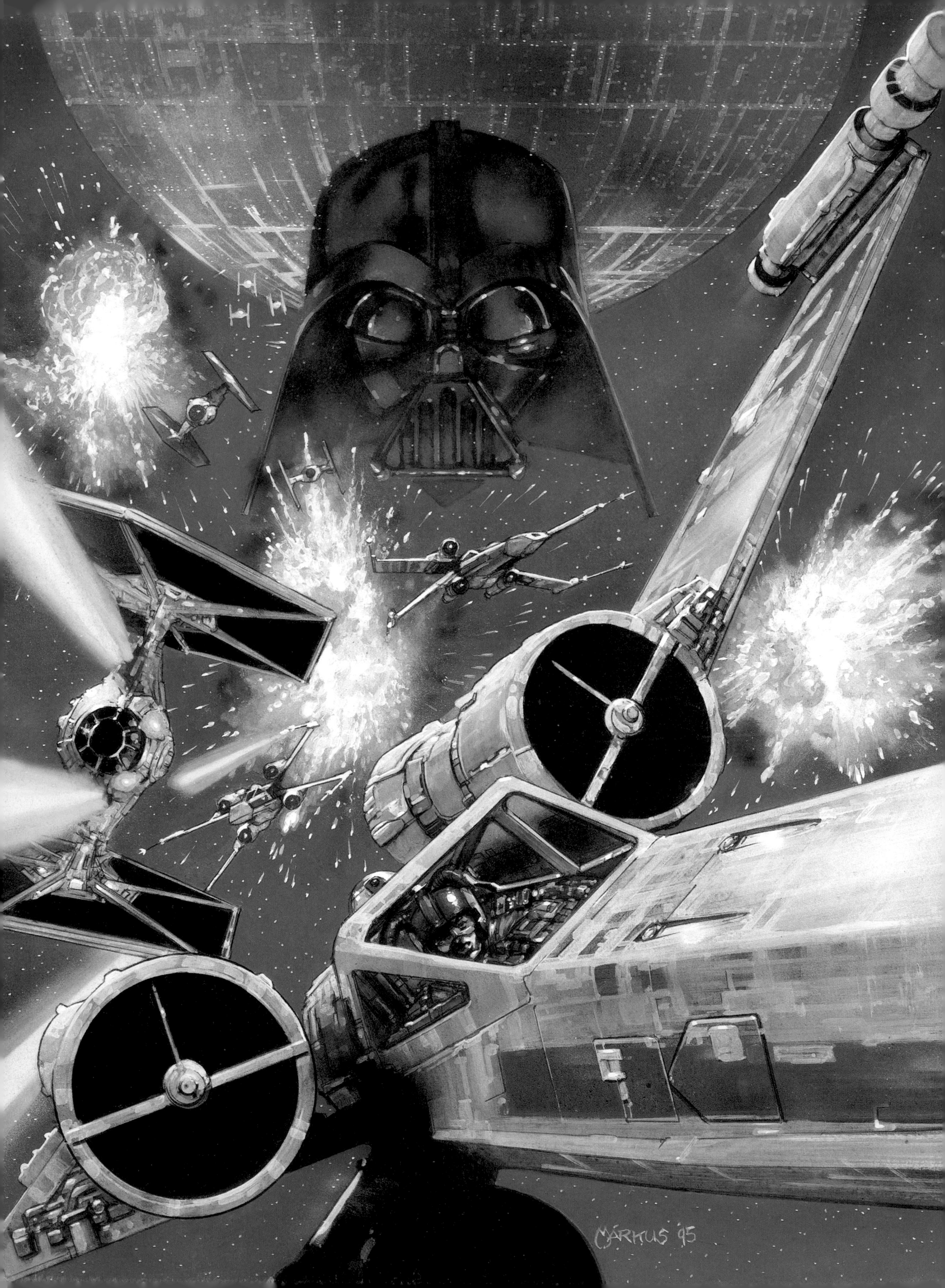
MÁRKUS '95

Work from the following artists appears on the nine-panel grids on pages 8, 24, 32, 49, 66, 82, 100, 114, 131, 146, and 164:

Brad Anderson, colors

Curtis Arnold, inks

Kia Asamiya, art

Michael Atiyeh, colors

Terry Austin, inks

Ramon F. Bachs, pencils

Brandon Badeaux, art

Eduardo Barreto, pencils

Ryan Benjamin, pencils

Edvin Biukovic, pencils

Patrick Blaine, art

Chris Blythe, colors

Dan Brown, colors

Paul Chadwick, art

Brian Ching, pencils

Chris Chuckry, colors

Will Conrad, art

Christian Dalla Vecchia, inks

Digital Broome, colors

Digital Chameleon, colors

Terry Dodson

Jan Duursema, pencils

Martin Egeland, pencils

Randy Emberlin, inks

Jordi Ensign, inks

Gary Erskine, art

Davidé Fabbri, pencils

Raul Fernandez inks

Manuel Garcia, pencils

Dave Gibbons, art

Tomás Giorello, pencils

Paul Gulacy, pencils

Tony Harris, art

Mark Harrison, art

Clayton Henry, pencils

HOON, art

Brian Horton, art

Christopher Ivy, inks

Dan Jackson, colors

Chris Justice

Cam Kennedy, art

Ryan Kinnaird, art

Ray Kryssing, inks

Fabio Laguna, inks

Mattieu Lauffray, art

Paul Lee, art

Rick Leonardi, pencils

Victor Llamas, inks

Guy Major, colors

Dave McCaig, colors

Angus McKie, colors

Harold McKinnon, colors

Carlos Meglia, art

Adriana Melo, pencils

Glen Murakami, art

John Nadeau, pencils

Ted Naifeh, art

Makoto Nakatsuka, art

Terese Nielsen

Neil Nelson, inks

Dave Nestelle, colors

Kevin Nowlan, inks

Jerome Opeña, art

Palmiotti Jimmy inks

Dan Parsons, inks

Andrew Pepoy, inks

Kilian Plunkett, art

Cary Porter, colors

Pamela Rambo, colors

Al Rio, pencils

Jasen Rodriguez, inks

Mel Rubi, pencils

P. Craig Russell, inks

Javier Saltares, pencils

Tsuneo Sanda, art

Mark Schultz, art

Eric Shanower, inks

Howard K. Shum, inks

C. P. Smith, pencils

Tom Smith, colors

Sno Cone Studios, colors

Chris Sprouse, pencils

Ken Steacy, colors

Dave Stewart, colors

Studio F, colors

Robert Teranishi, art

Greg Tocchini, pencils

Bodhi Tree, colors

Francisco Ruiz Velasco, art

Eddie Wagner, inks

Weems Joe inks

Doug Wheatley, pencils

Al Williamson, inks

Rick Zombo, pencils

STAR WARS COMICS TIMELINE (IN YEARS)

The Golden Age of the Sith—5,000 BSW4

Fall of the Sith Empire—5,000 BSW4

Knights of the Old Republic—4,000 BSW4

The Freedon Nadd Uprising—3,998 BSW4

Dark Lords of the Sith—3,997 BSW4

Sith War—3,996 BSW4

Redemption—3,986 BSW4

Jedi vs. Sith—1000 BSW4

Qui-Gon & Obi-Wan—38-37 BSW4

Jedi Council—33.5 BSW4

Darth Maul—33 BSW4

Republic—32-0 BSW4

Star Wars: Episode I—The Phantom Menace—32 BSW4

The Bounty Hunters—Aurra Sing—32+ BSW4

Jedi Quest—28 BSW4

Jango Fett—27 BSW4

Zam Wesell—27 BSW4

Starfighter—24 BSW4

Star Wars: Episode II—Attack of the Clones—22 BSW4

Jedi—22 BSW4

Droids—10-5 BSW4

Jabba the Hutt: Art of the Deal—5 BSW4

Underworld—1 BSW4

Classic Star Wars: Han Solo at Stars' End—10-0 BSW4

Boba Fett: Enemy of the Empire—3-0 BSW4

Empire—0 BSW4

Star Wars: Episode IV—A New Hope SW4

Vader's Quest—0+ ASW4

Classic Star Wars: The Early Adventures—0+ ASW4

River of Chaos—0+ ASW4

Classic Star Wars—0-3 ASW4

Shadow Stalker—0-3 ASW4

Splinter of the Mind's Eye—2 ASW4

Star Wars: Episode V—The Empire Strikes Back—3 ASW4

Tales From Mos Eisley—3 ASW4

Shadows of the Empire—3+ ASW4

The Bounty Hunters: Scoundrel's Wages—3+ ASW4

Star Wars: Episode VI—Return of the Jedi—4 ASW4

Jabba the Hutt: The Jabba Tape—4 ASW4

Mara Jade—4 ASW4

Shadows of the Empire—Evolution—4 ASW4

Classic Star Wars: The Vandelhelm Mission—4+ ASW4

X-Wing Rogue Squadron—4+ ASW4

Boba Fett: Twin Engines of Destruction—5 ASW4

Heir to the Empire—9 ASW4

Dark Force Rising—9 ASW4

The Last Command—9 ASW4

Dark Empire—10+ ASW4

Boba Fett: Death, Lies, and Treachery—10+ ASW4

Boba Fett: Agent of Doom—10+ ASW4

Empire's End—11 ASW4

Crimson Empire—11+ ASW4

The Bounty Hunters: Kenix Kil—11+ ASW4

Jedi Academy: Leviathan—13 ASW4

Union—20 ASW4

Chewbacca—25 ASW4

Old Republic Era
25,000 – 1000 years before
Star Wars: A New Hope

Rise of the Empire Era
1000 – 0 years before
Star Wars: A New Hope

Rebellion Era
0 – 5 years after
Star Wars: A New Hope

New Republic Era
5 – 25 years after
Star Wars: A New Hope

New Jedi Order Era
25+ years after
Star Wars: A New Hope

Infinities
Does not apply to timeline

BSW4 = before *Episode IV: A New Hope*. ASW4 = after *Episode IV: A New Hope*.